Transcultural Competence

Fundamentals of Consulting Psychology Book Series

APA FUNDAMENTALS OF CONSULTING PSYCHOLOGY

Transcultural Competence

NAVIGATING CULTURAL DIFFERENCES IN THE GLOBAL COMMUNITY

JERRY GLOVER AND HARRIS L. FRIEDMAN

AMERICAN PSYCHOLOGICAL ASSOCIATION • *Washington, DC*

Published by
American Psychological Association
750 First Street, NE
Washington, DC 20002
www.apa.org

To order
APA Order Department
P.O. Box 92984
Washington, DC 20090-2984
Tel: (800) 374-2721; Direct: (202) 336-5510
Fax: (202) 336-5502; TDD/TTY: (202) 336-6123
Online: www.apa.org/pubs/books
E-mail: order@apa.org

In the U.K., Europe, Africa, and the Middle East, copies may be ordered from
American Psychological Association
3 Henrietta Street
Covent Garden, London
WC2E 8LU England

Typeset in Minion by Circle Graphics, Inc., Columbia, MD

Printer: Edwards Brothers, Inc., Lillington, NC
Cover Designer: Naylor Design, Washington, DC

The opinions and statements published are the responsibility of the authors, and such opinions and statements do not necessarily represent the policies of the American Psychological Association.

Library of Congress Cataloging-in-Publication Data
Glover, Jerry.
  Transcultural competence : navigating cultural differences in the global community / Jerry Glover, PhD & Harris L. Friedman, PhD. -- First Edition.
    pages cm. — (Fundamentals of consulting psychology)
  Includes bibliographical references and index.
  ISBN 978-1-4338-1945-2 — ISBN 1-4338-1945-7 1. Culture and globalization.
2. Intercultural communication. 3. Cross-cultural studies. I. Friedman, Harris L. II. Title.
  HM621.G5976 2015
  303.48'2—dc23
                          2014037392

British Library Cataloguing-in-Publication Data
A CIP record is available from the British Library.

Printed in the United States of America
First Edition

http://dx.doi.org/10.1037/14596-000

Contents

Series Editor's Foreword

Rodney L. Lowman

The field of consulting psychology has blossomed in recent years. It covers the applications of psychology in consultation to organizations and systems but also at the individual and team levels. Unfortunately, there are very few graduate training programs in this field of specialization, so consulting psychology roles are mostly populated by those who came to the field after having trained in other areas of psychology—including industrial–organizational (I-O), clinical/counseling, and school psychology, among others. Yet such training is rarely focused on consulting psychology and psychologists, and graduate students have to learn through on-the-job training and by reading books and articles, attending conferences and workshops, and being mentored in the foundational competencies of the field as they seek to transition into it.

After a number of years of editing *Consulting Psychology Journal: Practice and Research*, the field's flagship journal, I felt that an additional type of educational product was needed to help those transitioning into consulting psychology. The Society of Consulting Psychology therefore partnered with the American Psychological Association and worked with an advisory board (initially consisting of Drs. Judith Blanton, Dale Fuqua, Skipton Leonard, Edward Pavur, Jr., and myself) to create a new book series describing the specific, fundamental skill sets needed to practice in this area of specialization. Our goal in this book series has been to identify the major competencies needed by consulting psychologists and then to work with qualified authors to create short, accessible but evidence-based texts that would be useful both as stand-alone volumes and in combination with one another. The readers would be graduate students in relevant training programs, psychologists planning a transition into consulting psychology, and practicing professionals who want to add to their areas of expertise.

What constitutes fundamental skills in consulting psychology? The educational guidelines created by the Society of Consulting Psychology and approved by the American Psychological Association (2007) and the *Handbook of Organizational Consulting Psychology* (Lowman, 2002) provide useful starting points. Both of these contributions were organized around the concept of levels (individual, group, and organizational) as a taxonomy for identifying fundamental skills. Within those categories, two broad skill sets are needed: assessment and intervention.

As with many areas of psychological practice, the foundational skills that apply in one area may overlap into others in the taxonomy. Interventions with individuals, as in executive coaching, for instance, usually take place in the context of the focal client's work with a specific team and within a specific organization, which itself may also constitute a client. Understanding the system-wide issues and dynamics at the organizational level usually also involves work with specific executives and teams. And multicultural/international issues suffuse all of our roles. The APA Guidelines and the *Handbook* concluded, properly, that consulting psychologists need to be trained in and have at least foundational skills and experience at the individual, group, and organizational levels, even if they primarily specialize in one of these areas.

In inviting you to learn more about consulting psychology through this book series, I hope you will come to agree that there is no more exciting or inherently interesting area of study today than consulting psychology. The series aims not only to cover relevant literature on timeless topics in consulting psychology but also to capture the richness of this work by including case material that illustrates its applications. Readers will soon understand that consulting psychologists are real-world activists, unafraid to work in real-world environments.

Finally, as one who trained in both I-O and clinical psychology, I should note that consulting psychology has been the one area in which I felt that all of my training and skill sets were both welcome and needed.

And in a world where organizations and the individuals and teams within them greatly need help in functioning effectively; in bridging individual, group, and organization-level needs and constituencies; and in coping with the rapid expansion of knowledge and escalating competition and internationalization, this book series aims to make a difference by helping more psychologists join the ranks of qualified consulting psychologists. Collectively, we can influence not only an area of specialization in psychology, but also the world.

ABOUT THIS BOOK

I can think of no better or more timely topic or book than *Transcultural Competence: Navigating Cultural Differences in the Global Community* to help launch the new Fundamentals of Consulting Psychology book series. Whether in providing feedback, assessment, coaching, team building, organizational consultation, or any of the large number of topics in which consulting psychologists must be competent, cultural and transcultural issues are almost always relevant. Yet, they are often overlooked. As this book makes abundantly clear, the contemporary version of cultural competence is not just about the important issue of cultural differences within a single country or area—it's also about becoming a transculturally competent global consultant (see Lopez & Ensari, 2013; Lowman, 2013).

Fledgling consulting psychologists may not aspire to international consulting careers, but aspects of international and multicultural consulting roles will affect them one way or another. With the rapid expansion of technology, coaching and assessment services are increasingly being delivered on a global scale. This may or may not be a good idea from the perspective of what we reliably know and do not yet know about such delivery methodologies, but the virtual revolution is proceeding with or without psychology, and it does provide consulting psychologists the opportunity to expand their services to persons who might not otherwise have access to them. And if these psychologists are going to consult all over the world, whether in person or online, then transcultural skills must be high on the list of "must have" competencies.

Glover and Friedman, the authors of this important book, have focused their life's work on transcultural issues in anthropology and psychology, respectively. In this volume, they distill this career-long work into its essence and incorporate theory (especially the work of Trompenaars and his associates; e.g., Trompenaars & Hampden-Turner, 2002), research, and illustrative case material to translate their wisdom into the most important points that consulting psychologists need to know to become transculturally competent consultants. The case examples, as wide ranging as whether U.S. military troops in a war zone should or should not smoke a hookah pipe with village elders and how an American fast-food restaurant should approach the design of its restaurants and menus in Japan, well illustrate the broader principles so that readers will quickly understand how important transcultural issues are to consulting psychologists. Indeed, consultants are always crossing cultural boundaries, even within their own cultures, because every organization they work with has a unique culture of its own, as do the groups and individuals within those organizations.

Transcultural Competence: Navigating Cultural Differences in the Global Community well illustrates the goals of the Fundamentals of Consulting Psychology book series. I expect that new consultants—and experienced ones as well—will be reading and applying this book for many years to come. It deserves that kind of attention and use.

Foreword

Fons Trompenaars

What an honor to be able to write a foreword to *Transcultural Competence: Navigating Cultural Differences in the Global Community*, a book that brings creativity and rigor to cultural training tools, models, and activities! I wholeheartedly agree with its authors on how important it is to make progress fast in this area. Further, the cry for transcultural rather than other approaches to cultural competence becomes louder during a time when we don't have to travel anymore to find an increasingly diverse population, and when training for a new type of cultural competence is needed more than ever. This book, therefore, is quite timely in bringing fresh perspectives to developing transcultural competence.

Jerry Glover and Harris L. Friedman show clearly the developments the cultural field has been going through and what learners need in order to develop transcultural competence. In the earlier chapters, a lot of attention is given to cultural understanding: What is culture, and how does it apply to me? Later parts of the book deal with cross-cultural and multicultural understandings leading to respect. Chapters then focus on how to deal effectively and appropriately with cultural differences and come to the core of what we call *transcultural competence.* Finally, Glover and Friedman provide insights on how to be careful with the cultural context that creates and influences cultural models and social institutions.

To further the discussion, it is interesting to see how this book aligns with the Transcultural Competence Profiler, which is completed online. For a free try, go to http://www.thtconsulting.com and use the password <Glover>.

Four major aspects of transcultural competence are discussed in this book:

Recognition: How competent is a person to recognize cultural differences around him or her? How we define ourselves, culturally speaking, is the focus that takes people on a learning journey to understand, articulate, and negotiate their cultural identities, which will help individuals respect cultural differences.

Respect: How respectful is a person about those differences? Respect serves as the basis for our attitudinal, cognitive, and behavioral orientation toward people who have diverse values. Stopping at the level of awareness and recognition might only support one's (negative) stereotypes as, if one has more knowledge/awareness of a particular culture, it could be used as more evidence for the negative stereotype. Respect for those differences is crucial for one's competence to deal with cultural differences. And one way of practicing respect is to understand that all human beings have the same dilemmas, but we approach those dilemmas in our particular cultural way.

Reconciliation: How competent is a person to reconcile cultural differences? I am very pleased that attention is given to going beyond understanding and respecting differences, as a key component of cultural competence is the ability to resolve differences. Glover and Friedman focus expressly on building the creative problem-solving skills required to navigate the complexities of various cultural situations. Isn't it a good idea that they included a section on dealing with dilemmas? Well done! It updates one of the most established arenas of this work with fresh thinking and ideas on how to best prepare people for cultural transitions.

Realization: How competent is a person to realize the actions necessary to implement the reconciliation of cultural differences? Activities such as building effective teams are among the ways to create realization. And one of the best ways we can help others is to continue to help ourselves in the journey toward transcultural competence.

I am delighted to see some parallel models with my own work and, even better, a set of practical tools to help professionals go beyond sheer adaptation and understanding of differences toward transcultural competence. I was also happily surprised and impressed by how much valuable thought and how many instrumental cases have been developed in all stages of this exploration of transcultural competence. I am hopeful that, with the work of Glover and Friedman, the coming years will be more progressive in dealing with the dynamics of the meeting of cultures, and go beyond just explaining that we are different. Best wishes in developing transcultural competence in others!

Preface

When the two of us agreed to write this book, we did so after over 30 years of collaboration on research, writing, and consulting. Harris was trained as a psychologist and Jerry as an anthropologist. We assumed that we might have different ideas and perspectives, but little did we realize the degree to which we understood and applied culture from different vantage points. This experience has reinforced our premise that the people who study and apply culture may not share explanations and methods. Eventually, we were able to reconcile our approach to explaining culture in this book.

Our book is largely based on the works of Drs. Fons Trompenaars, Peter Woolliams, and Charles Hampden-Turner. We are pleased to recognize and thank them for their leadership in the field of transcultural competence.

As an introduction to a general way of conceptualizing and practicing in a transculturally competent fashion, this book is written for professionals working across cultural divides, as well as any who interact within contexts influenced by culture—which means nearly everyone. Although it is part of a series directed toward consulting psychologists, it is written more broadly to be useful to any professional. It is also written in an accessible style with a minimum of professional jargon, and we have included numerous cases to illustrate how the need for transcultural competence exists around the global community. These cases are from culturally diverse contexts in many countries and across many organizational types.

Some are based on our own experiences and observations, while some come from others' work. Where indicated, we have changed the names of organizations, countries, and characters so they remain anonymous.

Our book uses the following organizational design. In the first two chapters, we discuss the need for transcultural competence and introduce our framework for understanding and applying culture. The next four chapters focus on the heart of our approach, which involves recognizing, respecting, reconciling, and realizing cultural differences. The next two chapters focus on professional disciplines and social institutions, whose relatively unrecognized cultural underpinnings we see as sources of frequent bias. This theme is continued in the next chapter, which focuses on recognizing and avoiding cultural traps. The final chapter summarizes our approach and presents some of its implications. We hope you will enjoy and benefit from reading this book, and we wish you the best in becoming more transculturally competent!

Transcultural Competence

1

The Need for Transcultural Competence

All men eat, but this is an organic and not a cultural fact. It is universally explainable in terms of biological and chemical processes. What and how different groups of men eat is a cultural fact explainable only by culture history and environmental factors. (Steward, 1972, p. 8)

The term *culture* is used at an ever-accelerating rate. Popular authors refer to the culture of a particular ethnic group when discussing social problems, sports announcers speak about the cultures of athletic teams, news analysts refer to the cultures of waste in governments, business pundits speculate about successful corporate cultures, and various professionals portray themselves as cultural experts. Almost everything is framed as cultural. It seems the growing use of this term has no end, as culture is finally being recognized as the significant influence on human experience and behavior that it has always been.

http://dx.doi.org/10.1037/14596-001
Transcultural Competence: Navigating Cultural Differences in the Global Community, by J. Glover and H. L. Friedman

CULTURE AND THE HUMAN EXPERIENCE

Steward's quote refers to the fact that there are cultural designs and patterns for eating in all human societies. For example, when people are hungry, they make decisions about when and where to eat, what to eat, with whom to eat, and even how to eat. So, if presented with an eating situation incongruent with their cultural values, people may choose not to eat, even though they are hungry. A vegetarian may choose not to eat meat, even if it is all that is available, due to cultural values. A Catholic may not eat meat on Fridays during Lent. A Muslim may fast during Ramadan. A New York maître d' may refuse to seat a customer in a restaurant, prohibiting eating, if a sufficient tip is not given in advance. Polynesians eat the eyes of fish as a delicacy, which most Westerners would refuse to even sample. The Maasai in Africa drink a mixture of milk and blood from their cattle, while in Thailand fried bugs are a commonplace snack sold on street corners. The examples of cultural differences in eating practices are endless. Eating practices are just one of many cultural patterns that vary around the globe and present the rich cultural diversity that characterizes humans.

Anthropologist Edward Hall (1981) emphasized the overwhelming importance of culture:

> Culture is man's medium; there is not one aspect of human life that is not touched and altered by culture. This means personality, how people express themselves, the way they think, how they move, how problems are solved, how their cities are planned and laid out, how transportation systems function and are organized, as well as how economic and government systems are put together and function. (pp. 16–17)

Culture is something humans have always dealt with. It is, and always has been, the means by which humans have met their daily needs and solved their problems of survival. For most of human history, culturally defined behaviors and practices by individuals and organizations have been assumed to be "the way things are done." Culture served as the agent of the status quo, with only the most creative and brave members of organizations and societies ever attempting to understand, manage, or change it.

It is reasonable to state that culture is actually what has made us human, at least in being able to solve the problems of human existence. Other species have also used culture, but only in very basic forms; no other living species has used culture as pervasively and successfully as humans: Culture influences everything humans do and experience (including our thoughts and emotions). Whether it is a stone axe or a computer, human technology is a cultural artifact. Likewise, social artifacts such as corporations, communities, and governments are organizations built and perpetuated from foundations of cultural knowledge. Leadership and other ways in which humans interact in organizations is the result of a specific cultural context. Culture is the foundation for organizing and managing all human groups through processes such as strategy, structures, systems, and technology, which lead to organizational outcomes (see Figure 1.1).

Yavi Rau

Human groups, organizations, and societies may develop different responses to the same needs. As an illustration of this process, different groups in Fiji

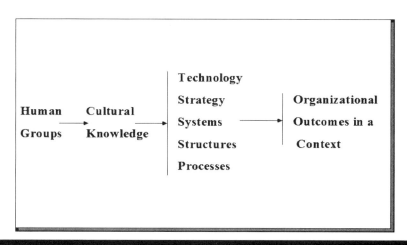

Figure 1.1

Culture and organizations.

meet some of their primary needs for obtaining sustenance through fishing, yet their secondary needs are based on varying Fijian cultural practices. In the Fijian society, there are Fijians, Fijian Indians who were originally brought to the islands as laborers, as well as expatriates from Australia, New Zealand, and other locations. Traditional Fijian culture has been based on communal village life, while the Fijian Indians' culture has been more individualistic and commercial. Australians, and other expatriates, bring their perspectives from their home countries, usually focusing on Western economic values and practices. Once when conducting a management-training seminar in Fiji, we asked our ethnically diverse participants to explain their cultural patterns for fishing. One manager jokingly provided the following explanation: "When villagers in Fiji fish, they use *Yavi Rau*, urban Fijians buy their fish in the market, Indians use one person with one fishing pole and five hooks, and the Australians pay someone to catch the fish for them." This humorous description given by the manager reflects different cultural models for doing the same activity, obtaining fish to eat. The cultural orientations of each of the four groups holding the models are quite diverse, as in the differing values toward individualism among the Australians, Fijian Indians, and urban Fijians, in contrast to the collectivism of the Fijians living in villages influenced by traditional communal values. Yavi Rau, the traditional Fijian fishing approach just mentioned, is very productive, even by modern Western standards when compared with the more individual methods for fishing. Most of the able Fijian villagers cooperate to catch fish. They go to a reef when the tide is receding, forming a human circle that forces the fish into a smaller area near the shore as the villagers move inward to shrink the circle. The fish are finally forced into a pool of water that, as the tide goes out, becomes small enough to allow the villagers to easily harvest the catch. Yet, we have heard those who do not share the traditional Fijian cultural model for fishing dismiss this as a "primitive" village practice. Such a bias from outsiders, denigrating a traditional practice that is actually quite productive, illustrates how cultural blinders can distort perceptions.

Transcultural Competence and Contemporary Professionals

Related to the term *culture* is the notion of competence in cultural matters, which is a learning progression that leads to what we call *transcultural competence*. Every human who lives as a member of a human society becomes culturally competent to the degree that he or she is socialized and learns to participate in a particular society. Humans first encounter culture when they learn their own cultural beliefs, patterns, and expected behaviors in daily living. That process of socialization is a two-edged sword: All humans learn how to survive and exist in their environment as they are socialized, but they also learn ethnocentric ways for dealing with the world around them, as all cultures tend to socialize their members to believe their ways are the best. So all humans learn a culture and, at the same time, learn that their culture's beliefs, patterns, and expected behaviors are correct, regardless of the specific culture into which they are born.

The next time humans may need to learn a culture is when they encounter other humans who do not hold the same cultural orientations. Some people may reject these new cultural orientations, while others may try to embrace them. At this point, those who learn a second cultural orientation may be seen as having cross-cultural competence, and they begin to develop a more advanced perspective on culture, leading to increasing recognition of cultural differences.

In today's culturally diverse global community, needs have emerged for many people to develop a third level of cultural learning called *multicultural competence*. This has become a well-recognized need for travelers, business executives, health care providers, government and community change leaders, mental health providers, educators, military professionals, and many others who deal with multiple cultures. In particular, it is becoming increasingly recognized that those people who communicate with and encounter many other cultures, both domestic and international, need to develop competence so that they can operate successfully when they cross multicultural boundaries. This includes a more heightened awareness of one's own culture as one way of doing things among many varying cultural possibilities.

The focus of this book is on a fourth level, namely, transcultural competence. This requires the learner to develop perspectives and skills for dealing with cultural differences that are beyond the first three levels described. Transcultural competence involves being able to adapt to various sociocultural settings anywhere in the world, with or without prior knowledge of the cultural orientations of those people and societies they are encountering. This general cultural adaptation requires more sophistication and a greater level of awareness and understanding of how culture works, regardless of the specifics of the sociocultural encounter.

Of the many professionals who employ the term *culture*, including those trained in the basic academic disciplines traditionally associated with culture (i.e., anthropology, psychology, and sociology), as well as those trained in various applied fields often dealing with culture (e.g., management, organizational behavior, organizational development), there is no shortage of people fashioning themselves as cultural experts. However, we have observed that few of these professionals claiming cultural expertise seem to really have a deep understanding of culture. Yet the need for understanding and applying knowledge of culture is pervasive across almost all professional disciplines. Transcultural competence, the ability to successfully deal with and develop solutions to issues and problems created by cultural differences within any cultural setting, is sorely needed in the contemporary global community.

Trompenaars (in Brotherton, 2011) referred to transcultural competence as going beyond being able to adapt to any specific culture, which can never be fully understood by a cultural outsider. Instead, transcultural competence involves being able to take advantage of diversity regardless of whether it relates to one specific culture or multiple differing cultures. Transcultural competence, according to Trompenaars, consists of four elements, which he called the "4Rs" of transcultural competence (see Figure 1.2):

> First, *recognition:* what is the dilemma? Second step is *respect:* there's a dilemma, and both sides have legitimate opinions. Third is *reconciliation:* the art of coming to some sort of agreement; the fourth is *realization:* actually translating it into actual behavior.

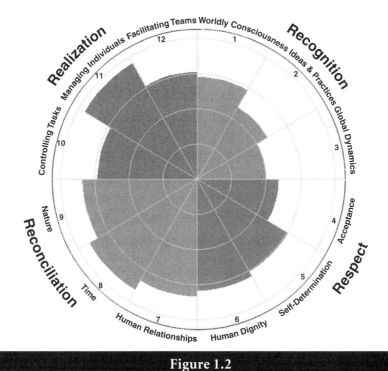

Figure 1.2

Four aspects of intercultural competence. From "Cross-Cultural Competence: Assessment and Diagnosis," by F. Trompenaars and P. Woolliams, 2006, *Adaptive Options, Spring*, p. 6. Copyright 2006 by Jerry Glover. Adapted with permission.

Transcultural competence enables those who possess it to recognize, respect, reconcile, and realize cultural dilemmas.

Psychologists, sociologists, anthropologists, organizational development and change professionals, management, and organizational behavior professionals, as well as educators, social workers, health care professionals, economists, and political scientists, are only a few of those needing transcultural competence. Social institutions in which professionals operate also need to foster transcultural competence, including business, government, health care, mental health, military, education, and community development. These are just a few of the many professional and institutional contexts in which there is a need to effectively apply cultural knowledge, regardless of location or situation. We provide the following cases to illustrate this need.

The New Waiter

Socialized values are in every organization, regardless of who their leaders are and what their approaches might be. In consulting in the Bahamas, we encountered an expatriate hotel manager who had inherited an organizational culture he did not understand. Having a successful management track record in England, he had been recently reassigned and asked for our assistance in solving labor problems at one of the hotel's restaurants. As he explained:

> We took over this restaurant three months ago. The former management company left us with a mess. Employees are surly, rude to customers, and close to a union walkout. Customers complain continuously about the service. Even our own hotel supervisors are afraid to go in there!

He was clearly baffled by the situation. The expatriate suggested that we continue the discussion while having lunch in the restaurant.

When we arrived at the restaurant, a young waiter warmly introduced himself and politely explained the menu options. As he walked away to place the order, Glover remarked to the manager, "I thought you said there were problems with the employees here, yet our waiter is doing everything you could expect for quality service." The manager grimaced and replied, "Yes he is, but today is his first day on the job. He has not yet learned to be like all the other employees."

Two weeks later, we returned to the restaurant for a follow-up meeting with the manager and encountered a very different response from the same waiter. He was not attentive, seemed unmotivated, and on one occasion bordered on rudeness. The waiter had obviously learned the behaviors of his more experienced coworkers. He now behaved like his other, less motivated, coworkers: He had become socialized as one of them.

The Western Businessman and the Arab Official

A business executive from the United States was working in a Middle Eastern nation to build a Western-style hospital (Copeland & Griggs, 1985). It was part of a community-development effort initiated by a local government. The executive went to a meeting with an Arab official to finalize the plans to open the hospital. During that meeting, he intended to obtain a permit from the official that would signify the government's approval to open the hospital. After arriving at the official's office, the executive appeared rushed and almost impatient with the official's insistence on making "small talk." He wanted to get to the point and appeared to anger the Arab official when he immediately asked for the permit to be signed. The American also was uncomfortable with the Arab official's multitasking activities, as the official answered his phone while speaking with the executive, was interrupted several times by his assistant, and was apparently not ready to discuss the permit until later in the meeting. The meeting ended without the permit being given to open the hospital. The executive was frustrated that the official did not share his urgency to open the hospital and expressed concern about how many people might not receive medical treatment due to this delay. But the official found the outsider to be rude and disrespectful of how things were done in that country. He was heard to say that his people had survived many years without this hospital, and they could survive a little longer.

Technology That Decreases Productivity

A casino-hotel general manager in Puerto Rico asked Glover to determine the cause of a "labor issue" in one of the property's restaurants. Upon his arrival, Glover spoke with the general manager to assess the problem. The general manager related that, for the past 6 months, what had historically been a well-managed and high-quality food outlet in the hotel had recently become a problematic and troublesome enterprise. Customer complaints regarding the service and the attitude of the employees had greatly increased during that period. Several long-time employees had resigned. Many others had complained about having too much work to do. There were even rumors of a possible grievance against management.

Glover next met with the waiters in the restaurant. After gaining their confidence, he learned from the waiters the source of their frustration in the workplace: "We work twice as hard now. Ever since the new computer (a point-of-sale terminal located in the customer service area) was installed six months ago, we don't have the time to do our jobs."

"But I thought the new technology was designed to make your life easier," Glover responded.

The waiters explained to him that since the new computerized system had been installed, they took the customers' orders, entered them in the terminal in the service area, and then went to the kitchen to tell the cooks what they had entered.

"Wait a minute," Glover responded. "Why do you have to go to the kitchen to tell the cooks what order you placed in the terminal? I thought they had a visual display terminal in the kitchen to tell them the orders placed from the service area."

After a few anxious moments, one of the senior waiters revealed the waiters' secret to him. "Yes, that is true, *but the cooks can't read.*" The waiters had been hiding the fact that the cooks, often their relatives or long-term friends, could not read. They feared the cooks might lose their jobs if this fact was discovered.

Multicultural Teams Provide Challenges

Friedman once served as a psychological consultant for a hospital where, to establish differential status and power across disciplines, a prominent neurosurgeon insisted on referring to him as "Nurse Friedman." This obvious attempt by the neurosurgeon to establish a favorable pecking order is an example of how the culture of that hospital was expressed in team meetings and how each discipline had its own culture. Health care organizations consist of many professional cultures. Patient care teams may include medical doctors, nurses, administrative staff, and social workers. In some cases, psychologists, occupational therapists, and other specialists may join these teams. Each of these health care specialists has a specific cultural approach, based on their socially defined roles, disciplinary education, credentialing process, and the shared expectations with others in their profession. To add to this, there may be a multicultural mix whereby the professionals and patients may be from different cultural backgrounds and approach the provider–patient relationship with different cultural orientations regarding health and well-being. In some cases, service providers and patients may not even share the same worldviews and beliefs about the nature of disease and acceptable treatments with Western-trained health care providers. These differences in worldviews and cultural values may be the source of problems, such as treatment team relationships, patient compliance, and medical malpractice.

Getting to Know You

In the 1980s, Glover worked as a consultant for Japan Airlines (JAL) when the company began to expand their hotel operations in North America. For 3 years, Glover went to the Essex House Hotel in New York City, the headquarters of the JAL hotel division, to serve as the consultant for a change process designed to transform the company from a Western management culture to a Japanese quality management system. During each visit to the headquarters, Glover had lunch with the JAL Development CEO for North America, Yasuki Muira. When they met for lunch at Spaghetti Lovers Pasta House each month, the conversation was never about the change initiative Glover was directing. Instead, the two discussed philosophy, politics, and other topics apparently unrelated to the change initiative. Finally, after a year of these lunch meetings, Glover asked, "Muira-san, why do we never discuss the project?" Muira smiled and said, "I have been getting to know you, your beliefs, your values, and how you think. If I like what I know about you, then I trust that you are doing a good job with the management culture changes." Glover found this leadership philosophy and approach to be quite different from those of the CEOs in the United States, who often focused on what was going to be done, when it would be done, what the results would be, and how much would it cost, while rarely wanting to establish a diffuse relationship with him. Muira, as a leader who had extensive multicultural experiences, is someone we consider to exemplify transcultural competence.

Western Notions of Progress May Not Be Shared

There are numerous cases to illustrate the need for understanding culture in the application of community development programs. Technology transfer, epidemiology, mental health, and literacy programs all have stake-holders with different, often competing cultural orientations. Add to that cultural mix the fact that development agents and political officials often have different values as well. For example, international aid projects have often provided what was thought to be an improvement, such as a trac-tor to increase farming yields or modern sanitation practices to better community health, only to find that these innovations were not adopted because they did not fit the local culture. A tractor might not fit into the collective work dynamics and might not have spare parts available to the farmers. Development agents would be disappointed to find, upon returning to a village after leaving a tractor with its farmers, that the trac-tor had not been used.

These cases illustrate the wide-ranging need to understand and work with cultural differences. Transcultural competence is important in all professions that work in the global community. We conclude Chapter 1 with a dilemma reported to us by U.S. soldiers operating in Afghanistan. This case illustrates how seemingly opposing values of participants in a meeting of culturally diverse stakeholders can have important implica-tions for all people involved in the situation.

CASE ANALYSIS: THE HOOKAH-PIPE DILEMMA

We recently elicited a perplexing dilemma from actual experiences of U.S. soldiers who had missions to build rapport with the elders of a traditional rural village in Afghanistan (Friedman et al., 2013). The village was located in an important area of a region occupied by so-called insurgents. Win-ning the support and cooperation of the village elders was critical to the security of the region. Also, the soldiers' immediate mission was to find weapons that were suspected to be hidden in the vicinity of the village.

When arriving to search for hidden weapons, the soldiers met with the elders, following the appropriate protocol for entering a village. After brief introductions, they were offered a hookah pipe by the Afghan elders. The interpreter explained that the elders would be insulted if they refused to participate in this ritual, but the pipe probably contained hashish, which is against U.S. military law. If soldiers did not smoke, then lives could be lost through not finding the hidden weapons, but to smoke could result in dire consequences for the soldiers via their own military-justice system.

When presented with this dilemma, members of all service branches in the focus groups were evenly split in their responses, with about half claiming they would have smoked and half that they would not have smoked from the pipe, suggesting it is a valid dilemma without a clear right or wrong answer. This dilemma involves the cultural-value dimension of specific-diffuse, namely, the soldiers might tend to express specific U.S. values to get down to business (as in finding the weapons), while the values of the elders might be more diffuse, demanding time to first build a trusting relationship through the hookah ceremony before revealing where the weapons were hidden. Further, should the soldiers decide to smoke or not smoke the hookah pipe, their commanding officer, and even the "brass" in the Pentagon, would hold their own values and expectations of how soldiers should respond in this culturally diverse situation.

Using cultural dilemmas provides a practical avenue to developing and employing transcultural competence, as well as for researching it. We have used dilemmas to assess, train, and intervene. For example, the hookah pipe dilemma was presented as one of the items in a dilemmas-based cultural-assessment instrument to military trainees with extensive experiences in international missions.

2

An Approach to Understanding and Applying Culture

We once were discussing culture and how to understand it with a group of mining engineers. One of the engineers posed the following question: "Culture seems very complex and difficult to comprehend; how do you seem to be able to explain it so easily?" The answer we gave was chosen to fit the engineer's worldview:

> You are a miner, and when you go into the mine you look at the structure and order that exists below ground. The strata levels reveal a picture to you of what is there. We study culture and, when we observe cultural patterns and social–cultural dynamics, we relate what we see to our understanding of the scenario, just as you relate to the strata to understand the mine below ground.

Culture is not easy to understand and apply, regardless of experiences and educational background. As members of a culture, people usually can only

http://dx.doi.org/10.1037/14596-002
Transcultural Competence: Navigating Cultural Differences in the Global Community, by J. Glover and H. L. Friedman

see the cultures of others through the lens of their own cultural orientations. For that reason, it is important to control for the biases of cultural orientation when attempting to understand cultural differences.

The need to avoid biases when understanding the diversity of human cultures is not new. Ethnographic records show that tribal societies usually divided people into "humans" and "nonhumans," with one's own society inevitably referred to as human and all others referred to as nonhuman. In 1537, the Catholic Pope decreed that Native Americans encountered in European explorations were indeed human (and not subhuman, as many Europeans had thought; Foster, 2009). So-called races were identified to categorize humans according to superficial physical traits, but the numbers of races and their defining characteristics have never been a scientifically valid concept. In the 19th century, anthropologists began to conduct ethnographic research, in particular on the tribal societies of the world, whereas in the 20th century, there were concerted attempts to make sense of all the ethnographic research (e.g., constructing the Human Relations Area Files; Murdock, 1967). Until the 1980s, most cultural research was conducted by anthropologists and sociologists, with some modest contributions by psychologists and other social scientists. During the 1980s, a surge of interest in culture occurred in management, organizational behavior, psychology, and other disciplines.

In more recent decades, this burgeoning interest in culture from management, organizational behavior, and psychology has been approached primarily from an individualistic vantage. A variety of concepts and methods for understanding culture, as well as various ways to understand cultural competence, have emerged from these efforts, as economic, political, military, and other human activities have increased the need to adapt to the newly emerging global community. The current situation is that most of these concepts and methods are limited in appropriateness by professional and disciplinary myopia toward the individual level of analysis. There has been a proliferation of self-report inventories, for example, which involve an individualistic focus and may not very effectively operationalize cultural variables (see Matsumoto & Van de Vijver, 2011). In fact, considering culture only from an individualistic perspective is itself congruent with Western cultural biases, as Western culture is known for being individualistic. Due to these disciplinary and Western biases, many concepts and methods are not culturally relative, and many do not adequately cover the range of human variation needed to be cultural–general. Fundamental to understanding and applying culture is the use of theories and methods appropriate for culture and its complexity.

We propose that the scientific study of culture is fundamentally necessary for developing valid and reliable perspectives (theories) and approaches (methods). There are three fundamental components in our approach to the understanding and application of culture. These are (a) identifying prerequisites for understanding culture; (b) using appropriate conceptual frameworks designed for making culture operational; and (c) developing methods that permit the collection and analysis of data with minimal biases from national, disciplinary, institutional, and other limiting perspectives.

PREREQUISITES FOR UNDERSTANDING AND APPLYING CULTURE

It is fundamental that any approach to understanding and applying culture reflect an understanding of prerequisites needed to effectively define and operationally use culture. These prerequisites are taken from the research on culture from the past 150 years. Most of this research on culture has been generated by anthropologists and, to a lesser extent, sociologists, and eventually by other social, organizational, and behavioral scientists. Theories and methods for the understanding and application of culture that do not start with these prerequisites are likely to be conceptually flawed and methodologically biased in how they deal with culture.

Cultural Relativity

The first prerequisite for the scientific study of culture involves embracing *cultural relativity*, which means not privileging any cultural difference as being inherently better or worse. Privileging one way as being best when that singular way happens to be that of one's own culture constitutes *ethnocentrism*. Ethnocentrism is often the reason for professional and disciplinary biases in the way culture is defined and operationalized. One of the best ways to grow beyond ethnocentrism is by gaining experiences in different cultures, which can lead to recognizing one's own culture more clearly, as well as recognizing and respecting the cultures of others.

It is equally important to understand the range of human variation. For example, when attempting to understand economic exchange behavior, it is important to be able to explain how the three widely recognized methods for economic exchange (reciprocity, redistribution, and the market principle) vary in different contexts around the world. In some human societies relying on subsistence economies, reciprocity and redistribution are prominent, while the market principle is not as important. However, in most contemporary societies, the market principle has become the most prominent form of economic exchange. Why is this important? Because if we are interpreting economic exchanges in a rural village in Africa, armed with our Western belief in the market principle of exchange, then most likely our interpretation of the behaviors of villagers influenced primarily by reciprocity and redistribution would be biased.

Synchronic and Diachronic Perspectives

Synchronic perspectives look at people in the present broadly across space (e.g., cross-culturally), whereas *diachronic* perspectives look at people throughout time (e.g., through tradition and history). As an example, understanding how humans make decisions requires looking across different cultures (using a synchronic perspective), which includes an understanding of decision making used by all humans, not just those taken from one culture. When decision making is observed across the continuum of human culture that exists in the contemporary global community, a wide range of cultural perspectives and practices for making decisions are found. For example, an expatriate from the United States who wants to negotiate a contract in locations such as Japan, China, or the Middle East may become very frustrated because the contractual models from the

United States for negotiations and decision making are not practiced in those different cultural settings.

In addition, cultures do not arise in a vacuum, but always have a historical context. Another prerequisite to understanding and applying culture is developing a sense of how things became what they are, not just paying attention to what they are in the present. A diachronic perspective allows for a look across time. In cultures that privilege the present and future at the expense of the past, as in much of the United States, there are temporal limitations for deep understanding. It also should be kept in mind that cultures change continuously over time. For example, not understanding the pre-Colonial past of many developing nations may lead an outsider to misunderstand the current political and ethnic divisions that may exist today. Pre-Colonial political and spatial boundaries in countries such as Nigeria were very different from the post-Colonial nation now referred to as Nigeria. In the present, numerous traditionally independent societies, with different languages and cultures, are now considered one nation-state and are expected to coexist in their new political and spatial boundaries—but this does not always work out well.

Holistic Perspectives

Having a view in which all aspects of a culture are taken into consideration is another prerequisite to understanding and applying culture. A culture's economic, political, religious, and other institutions are all crucial to consider. Focusing only on one-dimensional variables, such as currently observed behavior, lacks *holism*. Without holistic perspectives, professional researchers and practitioners may not realize the obvious, that the "whole is greater than the sum of its parts." In cultures, it is especially important to recognize that components are always interrelated. In fact, relationships may hold more importance than any specific cultural components in understanding culture and cultural differences. A failure to see the "bigger picture" in a cultural context may lead to unanticipated consequences, faulty theoretical perspectives, and flawed methods for understanding culture and how it works. For example, installing the point-of-sale terminals in the Puerto Rican restaurant discussed in Chapter 1 required integration into the workplace context. This focus only on the technology, without consideration of the sociocultural situation, led to the initial failure of the system designed to increase productivity.

APPROPRIATE FRAMEWORKS FOR MAKING CULTURE OPERATIONAL

For over a century, the fields of anthropology and, to a lesser extent, sociology have focused on understanding culture from the perspective of value dimensions. They have also emphasized the prerequisites we have discussed: cultural relativity, both synchronic and diachronic perspectives, and holism. In this regard, values can be seen as composed of common dimensions, which can provide a framework for understanding culture. In addition, cultural values are always expressed when people interact, which provides a way to scientifically approach culture.

Cultural-Values Dimensions

Cultural values are essentially what is important to people. Values are embedded in the worldviews, beliefs, and paradigms held by people from different societies, organizations, ethnic groups, and other social arrangements. We use Trompenaars and Hampden-Turner's (2002) 7D model to provide our framework for cultural-values dimensions. This model includes the values of individual–collective, universal–particular, and specific–diffuse, and also achievement–ascription, neutral–affective, internal–external, and time (sequential–synchronic and past–present–future). These values dimensions can be used in a transcultural way to observe, understand, and analyze human behavior in any setting, regardless of the location and context. Understanding these is another prerequisite for applying culture in the pursuit of transcultural competence.

We provide a more detailed description of cultural-values dimensions in Chapter 4. For our immediate discussion, we illustrate the universal–particular and specific–diffuse dimensions. *Universal* values involve wanting everything to be uniform, without exceptions. For example, a discipline's focus on finding "laws" that account for all cultural differences illustrates universalism, while particularism would involve respecting exceptions based on the local-cultural context. *Specific* values refer to setting clear boundaries, such as separating business from social roles, while *diffuse* values refer to allowing more permeable boundaries, as in treating business associates like family.

Sociocultural Encounters

A sociocultural encounter (SCE) occurs in any situation in which social actors meet with other social actors. Each SCE has a context, stakeholders with cultural-values orientations that may differ, as well as various other dynamics, such as power differentials. These hold the potential for generating cultural dilemmas. We consider the concept of SCE as a means for providing a culturally relative conceptual framework, since there are no absolute right or wrong answers in dealing with dilemmas arising in SCEs (e.g., in the Hookah-Pipe Dilemma presented in Chapter 1), but there is only what does or does not work within a given cultural context. During SCEs in which cultural dilemmas need to be handled, certain performances of actors may be more or less adaptive, but these are not based on any rote application of simple rules. In brief, SCEs provide an entrée to better conceptually frame and understand culture without either losing relevance or imposing one's own cultural biases.

All human interactions take place within an SCE. For example, early humans began to develop cultural knowledge as a means for adapting to a variety of ecological and social contexts. SCEs were the location and means by which early language, social relations, and cooperative activities among band and tribal members developed. SCEs were the settings for human knowledge acquisition and transfer within and across societies. SCEs became the platform for subsistence acquisition and sharing, economic exchanges, kinship, socialization, conflicts, and all the activities recognized as human culture. Further, worldviews, beliefs, and values formed the basis for actors' behaviors within SCEs. Lastly, SCEs provide opportunities for observation and replication, allowing a scientific approach to understanding and applying culture.

METHODS THAT MINIMIZE BIASES

Using a cultural-dilemmas approach, and SCEs in which stakeholders with seemingly opposing values interact, provides a practical avenue toward understanding and applying culture, as well as researching it. Dilemmas can be used to both assess and intervene in SCEs in culturally diverse settings.

The methods we present derive from long-standing anthropological and sociological traditions, meet the prerequisites identified as necessary for culturally valid scientific work, and are grounded in the cultural-values dimensions. We also use SCEs to scientifically operationalize our approach through employing both qualitative and quantitative, as well as other (e.g., graphical) approaches to gathering and analyzing data through what we call *cultural metrics.* Theories and methods for transcultural competence must be appropriate for any local situation, yet have relevance across all of humanity, to be valid.

Our approach meets the prerequisites for validity in researching and working with culture, as it is culturally relative, both synchronic and diachronic, holistic, and involves values dimensions. SCEs provide opportunities for gathering data that meet the generally accepted standards of science (e.g., observability, minimizing biases, replicability), while cultural-values dimensions provide the framework from which we interpret SCEs.

Cultural dilemmas occur, and can be observed, during SCEs in which actors with different and often competing and even conflicting worldviews, beliefs, and values engage. These dilemmas involve cultural differences that are often not well understood by the actors involved. They may approach the dilemma from their ethnocentric vantages, while being relatively blind to the vantage point of the other. SCEs are fundamental to our approach to culture, but it is the concept of cultural dilemmas that holds the real power during SCEs. The outcome of SCEs in which cultural dilemmas need to be handled provides our way to approach culture operationally. Also, when cultural dilemmas are handled successfully, this reflects high transcultural competence in that context. This SCE and dilemmas approach is culturally relative in that what might work well within one cultural context might fail abysmally in another, so there are no right or wrong ways to demonstrate transcultural competence. Instead, there are adaptive behaviors (Glover, Friedman, & Jones, 2002) that work within the SCE and involve interactional attributes. Transcultural competence leading to reconciling and realizing beneficial results with cultural dilemmas within SCEs is essential. Cultural dilemmas are found in all sociocultural contexts, and are particularly relevant in culturally diverse situations.

CASE ANALYSIS: DOES YOUR VISION MATCH REALITY?

Corporate, government, and community leaders often develop vision statements in the belief that it will result in improving the performance of employees. That may or may not be the case in specific organizations. However, for these vision statements to be effective, they need to be experienced as being real by the employees and consumers, and not just seen as empty rhetoric.

We conducted an organizational culture project involving the merger of a financial services company with a government-owned bank in the South Pacific. The cultural-dilemmas method had been used to assess the cultural values among stakeholders and functional areas in both organizations. Our goal was to use the data from the assessment to anticipate potential merger problems and to create appropriate change initiatives to smooth the transformation. In other words, we conducted a "cultural due diligence" assessment for the merger.

The content of the assessment had been based on cultural dilemmas elicited in focus groups and interviews in both the financial services company and the bank. After constructing and administering a cultural-dilemmas instrument, as part of a battery of assessments, we met with the executives of the newly merged organization to present the results.

As we arrived at the venue for the meeting, we noticed a large banner draped on the wall. It stated the newly formed company's vision, which the executives had developed in a consultant-led retreat the previous weekend. The CEO proudly told us that the new vision statement would be the guiding influence on the merger as it progressed. The vision was simple and well stated: "We will be the leader in our region in providing quality financial solutions which exceed our customers' expectations." The executives appeared to be quite happy with the statement until we raised the issue of a dilemma identified in the cultural-merger assessment.

One of the cultural assessment items asked staff from both companies to address this dilemma: "A long-standing and important customer walks into a sales office and requests an exception to the loan limit on his existing insurance policy. What action should be taken with the customer's request?" When we reviewed the responses given, we found some interesting differences between functional areas in the company. Accountants in both companies had chosen the response "Do not approve the exception," while sales and marketing staff had chosen the response "Give the exception."

The problem presented to the executives of both merging organizations was not just the different responses, but matching the reality of this dilemma to the new vision statement. It became obvious to the executives that they would need to do more than just post an aspirational banner in their meeting room. They needed to find ways to make the vision operational in the workplace with the company's interactions with its customers. If they met the customers' needs, many of the fiscal policies developed to manage the company might have to be changed. On the other hand, if they held the line and denied the customer's request for an exception, they would be disingenuous to their vision.

This universal–particular cultural dilemma illustrates a common problem faced by many leaders. There are no clear solutions. It involves the universal value that the "rules are the rules" without exception, as opposed to a particular value that catering to a specific customer evidences good customer services. It is no surprise that the accounting staff preferred the former position, while those in sales and marketing preferred the latter.

By working with such values conflicts, organizational culture can be accurately assessed. Appropriate interventions, such as working to align vision statements to the reality of the day-to day operations of an organization, can be used to reconcile and realize positive outcomes involving dilemmas. Clarifying techniques include identifying values, stakeholders, and other important aspects of the dilemma without imposing any right answer.

This case also illustrates the importance of developing ways to operationalize visions and missions in organizations. Nice-sounding statements, often developed by consultants and organizational leaders, mean nothing if the values expressed in the visions and missions cannot be operationalized. Cultural dilemmas and SCEs provide a method to operationalize such statements.

3

Recognizing Cultural Differences

The location is a village in Afghanistan. A group of three U.S. soldiers and an interpreter have entered the village. While visiting the village, one of the soldiers is encouraged to remove his helmet and sunglasses by a young woman. She giggles and playfully shows interest in the soldier. He returns the interest and gestures for her to remove her veil. She removes her veil to reveal her face. Unexpectedly, the woman's younger brother sees her without her veil. He is appalled, and begins to beat her with a stick. The girl's father hears the disturbance and comes out of his house. There is a volatile situation as the father is angry and tells the interpreter that the soldier did not respect his daughter. The interpreter is able to calm the father and brother. A discussion ensues in which the problem is debated by the villagers and the soldiers.

This story, told to us by U.S. soldiers who actually encountered this situation, illustrates stakeholders with seemingly opposing cultural values

http://dx.doi.org/10.1037/14596-003
Transcultural Competence: Navigating Cultural Differences in the Global Community, by J. Glover and H. L. Friedman

in an SCE—a cultural dilemma. It is relatively easy for outsiders from the West to view the behaviors of the woman's younger brother and father as wrong. From the villagers' cultural orientation, it is easy to see the soldiers as not respecting the daughter and the family.

The terms *emic* and *etic* are used for differing perspectives of cultural insiders and outsiders, respectively. Using Afghanistan as the cultural referent, an emic perspective comes from a person embedded within the culture, such as the Afghan girl's brother and father, whereas an etic perspective comes from the outsider to the culture, such as the U.S. soldiers. Although the etic perspective may attempt to be "objective" or "culturally neutral," such etic perspectives always come from someone's own cultural perspective.

This flirting between the girl and the soldier could have been the spark that ignited a conflict between the Afghan villagers and the soldiers. Or it could have been resolved to minimize potential problems, with its outcome dependent on the transcultural competence of one or more of the stakeholders. The essence of being transculturally competent is to be able to adaptively respond in such encounters in a manner that leads to a mutually satisfactory resolution to the situation. Being able to deal with the cultural diversity of stakeholders in SCEs like the flirting case is expected from a transculturally competent professional.

As we discussed in Chapter 1, recognizing, respecting, reconciling, and realizing cultural differences, within the context of the prerequisites we described, are all fundamental to developing transcultural competence. This chapter presents a framework for such a working knowledge of culture. Recognizing cultural differences is the first, and most fundamental, step in the four-step process. Recognition begins with a general understanding of what culture is and how it works.

GENERAL FEATURES OF CULTURE

Culture provides basic elements for survival and solving the problems of human existence. These elements are essential to all societies and human groups, no matter how large or small, simple or complex, or different in any way.

Culture Provides Meaning to the World

All humans perceive the world around them through a cultural lens. Meaning is given by interpreting a sociocultural context using worldviews, beliefs, and values. For example, a meeting involving culturally diverse actors may have the same physical context for all stakeholders, but perceptions, what is valued, and how a stakeholder behaves may be based on very different cultural orientations. Events such as meetings, ceremonies, negotiations, and communications all involve cultural interpretations of reality.

Culture Is Shared and Learned

Cultural knowledge is collectively used by specific societies and social groups to respond to the needs and problems of existence. Every human group has means for socializing its members. Socialization provides for continuity through generations. In workplaces and organizational cultures, new employees learn the behaviors and expectations of their new environment. Professionals learn the worldviews and values of their disciplines. Essentially, each socialization process provides guidelines for how to see the world, how to respond in SCEs, and what is valued. In early homogeneous human societies, socialization may have been informally based on oral traditions and imitation of others. In more contemporary heterogeneous societies, socialization may be based on both informal and formal means. In both cases, families, peer groups, and communities are involved. Schools and corporate training programs illustrate more contemporary institutions for socialization. Mass media, including television, movies, music, and social media, are also part of socialization in most countries today.

Culture Is a Process

Culture is not static, frozen at a point in time. Consider that humans interact in a series of action chains (Bohannan, 1995). These action chains involve processes in which people allocate time and resources and set priorities in response to their social and physical environments (Barth, 1967).

This fact is particularly important in cultural change. Planned change efforts, if they involve more than superficial activity and temporary attention, involve people reallocating their time, resources, and priorities to align with the change initiative. Even in situations with minimal changes planned, the continuation of things as they have been in the past involves processes that support the status quo. Change is a process in which people reallocate how they spend their time, set priorities, and use resources.

Reincorporating the Cultural Prerequisites

Culture is not just a collection of independent parts; instead, it is holistic. Culture is an integrated system, including its structure, its relationships among its components, as well as its technology. More specifically, human organizational forms, such as a corporation, health care facility, mental health center, school, and neighborhood, are cultural systems of meaning, technology, relationships, and people. For example, family and kinship can best be understood if their relationship to the economic, political, and ideological components of a society is known.

The context, including the physical, social, and historical environments, is important. Culture needs to be framed in both diachronic and synchronic perspectives. Cultural values provide dimensions for understanding human variation in a culturally relative perspective. While few humans hold values in the extremes of cultural dimensions, dimensions do provide limits to the range of human variation. For example, when we consider humanity in a globally appropriate perspective, humans may be prone to value individualism or they may be prone to value collectivism. However, no human has been observed to demonstrate values outside of the individual–collective continuum. Just as all people eat, with the details of their eating being culturally variable, all people generally behave somewhere on the individual–collective continuum, but how they behave on that continuum varies. Therefore, cultural-values dimensions permit the understanding of human experience in ways that are universal and that also avoid privileging any single expression as being better or worse on the continuum, and therefore are culturally relative.

Social Institutions

Early ethnographers developed accounts of the peoples being studied by analyzing functional aspects of culture—their social institutions. Focusing on these institutions provided a means for collecting and organizing ethnographic data to understand the wide range of human culture and its evolution. There are many social institutions that have evolved and are expressed differently across cultures, which include economic, kinship and affiliation, political, technological, ecosystem, and ideological institutions, as well as others. Understanding these institutions and being able to work within them is fundamental to recognizing cultural differences.

Economic Behaviors

Economic institutions include human activities used to provide food and other necessary resources for survival. As cultural evolution led to more complex divisions of labor and social stratification based on food domestication, human economic institutions experienced significant transformations. The nomadic existence of bands and tribes was the primary means of survival until around 10,000 years ago, when people moved toward more sedentary urban patterns, including the beginnings of the idea of ownership of land and other forms of private property. As humans were more able to produce food, instead of extracting food as bands and tribes did, specialists also developed as social groups and became capable of producing food beyond the immediate needs of food producers. Excess food production supported these new social classes and specialists. All of the emerging human economic activities set in place a process that eventually led to the current prevailing urban economies in which most of the populations are not involved in food production. Instead, most humans are now specialists, often far removed from the daily activities of producing food. If all the adaptive knowledge of urban culture were to be suddenly removed, most humans today would not survive for long. Changing from food extraction to food production was the impetus for modern human cultural evolution via the institutions of economics.

Another aspect of cultural evolution related to economics involved the transition from a general division of labor to a complex division of labor. Homogeneous societies, in particular, bands, tribes, and chiefdoms, were mainly organized into a general division of labor based on gender and age. As cultural evolution led to more complex economic activities, including being driven by innovations in technology, more complex divisions of labor emerged. Specialists, including those with knowledge of predictive sciences needed for food production, became important. Specialists were supported by the food producers. Social control and protection of the crops and land needed for mass food production were supported by developing a military class.

Although many interested in culture might not emphasize the importance of economics, from a diachronic perspective this is a major aspect of culture's origin. Because economic systems vary widely today, understanding its synchronic effect on culture is equally important. The same can be said for all of these fundamental social institutions.

Kinship and Affiliation Behaviors

Kinship and affiliation institutions include both biological and social means for cooperation and survival. In homogeneous societies, kinship groups were the basis for social organization. Everyone was somehow related to everyone else in the society. Identity was associated with kinship and lineage. All cultural institutions, such as economic institutions, were closely integrated with kinship. They were all interdependent, part of an integrated system for providing meaning to the members of society.

As cultural evolution has led to more complex, heterogeneous societies, there has been a trend toward compartmentalizing cultural institutions. For example, the transition from rural to urban societies led to a breakdown of the traditional three-generational family residing in the same household within the United States, leading to the nuclear or even single-parent families often found today as newer social forms of this institution.

In contemporary societies, the strains between traditional kinship practices and more compartmentalized institutions have led to inconsistent and confused means for meeting affiliation needs and forging identity. Alienation and anomie have become common. For example, in the United States, gangs and other peer groups play an important role in the socialization of children and youth, replacing the need for belonging, previously met by the family. Likewise, the elderly, ill, and needy are frequently put in "warehouses" for care to replace the generalized human service support systems characteristic of earlier societies. Even schools can be seen as warehouses that may be underfunded and have deep problems, such as violence and poor academic outcomes. Adults often now forge their strongest identities through their work, in which their vocational affiliations replace traditional family ties.

Political Behaviors

Political institutions include means for social control, governance, conflict resolution, and the use of power. They are closely tied to economic systems, frequently justifying economic disparities as legitimate under laws. Early human societies were based on consensual political institutions, as kinship was typically the basis for political activities. As cultural evolution led to more complex and heterogeneous societies, coercive power and institutionalized social control in the form of military and other specialists also developed. Ownership of land, property, and other resources led to "haves" and "have-nots," as well as other expressions of social and economic classes. Egalitarian early human societies evolved toward societies based on unequal access to goods and services, enforced by a political order.

Cultural evolution related to politics led to changes in the forms of production and economic exchanges, as explained through the works of Adam Smith (1904), Karl Polanyi (1944), and Karl Marx (1992). In the Colonial era, economic exchange based on redistribution and reciprocity were most prevalent in the non-Western world. The market principle, based on the exchange of goods and services according to market price, was an alien concept to many peoples in the world who encountered the colonialists from Europe and, later, from North America. These new institutions were often imposed on those colonized through the use of force. The Colonial Era transition from reciprocity and redistribution to the market principle had far-reaching political ramifications. The trio of capitalism, colonialism, and Christianity (the 3Cs) was the equivalent to a steamroller in many non-Western societies. Increasingly, European powers were able to dominate politically and militarily due to the 3Cs and other influences, such as the non-Westerners' lack of previous exposure to European diseases. In the contemporary world, it is still common to find people in various parts of the world struggling with issues directly stemming from this great political, economic, and social change. Many peoples have been faced with dilemmas of private property versus collective ownership, sharing versus individual consumption, and traditional local power dynamics versus a global system of Neocolonial power and influence.

Technology-Related Behaviors

Institutions related to technology include the manufacture and use of human tools and related artifacts. In early human societies, technology was expressed in stone tools, simple shelters, and clothing. All of these were related to food extraction, protection, and shelter. Cultural evolution has led to a complex array of human tools, such as aircraft, automobiles, electronic appliances, computers, and mobile devices. The range of human applications has gone far beyond food extraction, protection, and shelter. Technology has extended the knowledge available to humans, greatly increased the range and frequency of human communication, and enabled possibilities for activities never before considered in early human societies, such as space travel.

On the other hand, technology has created problems in the human experience. Pollution, sedentary lifestyles, wars for the control of oil and other resources needed for systems of production and consumption can be linked to technology and its pervasive control over most urban societies. Technology, as with other cultural institutions, is continuously evolving diachronically, but it remains diverse in its expression from a synchronic perspective. As humans have evolved from stone tools to computers and high-rise buildings, technology is an integral component of cultures.

Ecosystems and Behavior

Ecosystem dynamics include relationships of human societies to physical and social environments. This includes the ongoing interaction of political, economic, and technological human activities in natural environments. Humans have evolved from early societies in which substantive economics and available technology imposed limits, based on resources available for extraction from the physical environment, controlling population growth and other pressures on the environment. In addition, cultural beliefs and values placed humans as part of their environments. Contemporary societies, in contrast, are often based on mass consumption, exponential population growth, and cultural values and beliefs that humans are the masters, and not merely a part, of their environments. Instead of being integrated parts of the ecosystems, humans are altering the planet in ways that may not be sustainable, while cultural evolution has gone beyond the constraints of biological evolution.

Ideology and Behaviors

Institutions involving ideology include those related to the worldview of a society. These ideology-based institutions have a profound impact on all other institutions, but may be the most difficult to see for those who hold tightly to their ideological commitments. In early human societies, ideology was integrated into the overall way that people saw the world, as everyone essentially shared the same beliefs and ways of giving meaning to the world around them. Cultural evolution eventually led to the beginning of predictive science. The mix of the sacred and the secular characterizes the ideology of most cultures today. Ideology based on the sacred is still very important in contemporary societies, even when the secular is also important.

Science is part of ideology. As with sacred ideologies, science has its beliefs, as explained by Thomas Kuhn (1962). Ideology can be an important influence in other social institutions, such as economics, as explained by Max Weber (1930). Ideology based on the secular can include political beliefs and models, such as communism (Marx, 1992) and capitalism (Smith, 1904).

At the organizational level, it is common to observe corporate visions and other expressions of ideology. Organizational leaders develop ideologies that reflect their beliefs and values and attempt to instill those beliefs and values in their employees. It is also possible to find religious influences in the cultures of organizations. For example, banks in the West charge interest freely and openly as a way of doing business. In Islamic societies, banks often still follow the belief that charging interest is inappropriate and violates their religious beliefs.

LEVELS OF CULTURE

Culture has different levels of meaning. These levels include behaviors, systems and processes, and values, beliefs, and worldviews. Understanding how humans solve problems, and how different human groups have developed different adaptive responses, requires some means for analyzing these levels.

Behavioral Level

This is the most basic level of cultural meaning. More superficial and obvious levels include behaviors that can be observed, such as the differing office designs in Tokyo, London, and Miami. Other behaviors include how people dress, the way they talk, and the nature of their relationships with others. Behaviors might also include interactions with a computer network or the way guests are checked into a hotel. The behavioral level is where most contemporary Western leaders focus when trying to manage an organization, understand it, or change it. Unfortunately, this level is not sufficient to get at the root causes of behaviors. Instead, the deeper levels of cultural meaning that lie beneath the surface of behaviors need to be considered for transcultural competence.

Systems Level: Structures, Technology, Strategies, and Processes

Less obvious levels of the meaning of culture include the systems and processes that structure peoples' behavior in given situations. For example, change initiatives such as reengineering, quality improvement, technology transfer, and joint ventures are all based on cultural-design orientations for how things in an organization should be done. In a change project, the existing cultural designs (tradition) are to be replaced or modified by the new cultural designs (the innovation). When the old and the new cultural designs create dilemmas that are not reconciled and realized, the possibility of change failure is greatly increased.

Thus, it is very difficult to successfully implement change unless the systems level is adapted to the expectations of the champions of the new initiative. At the same time, it is also necessary for key stakeholders to perceive that the change model has relative advantage, within their models for explaining and giving meaning to the world.

Values Level

The deeper levels of culture are not easy to understand for many who wish to become transculturally competent. These levels include values and beliefs (i.e., worldviews). At these levels of cultural meaning, humans hold culturally prescribed assumptions that influence the way they see the world.

For example, Andre Laurent (1983) described how values influence the way things happen in organizations. He showed that business leaders from different national cultures hold different assumptions regarding the nature of management and organization. These different sets of assumptions shape different value systems and get translated into different management and organizational practices that, in turn, reinforce the original.

As another example of the influence of cultural values, Trompenaars (in Brotherton, 2011) stated, "Did you know that about 90 percent of the books on leadership are written by Anglo-Saxons? And I have nothing against Anglo-Saxons, but only five percent of the world lives there. Individual countries often have their own definition and books on leadership."

Beliefs Level

The deepest level of meaning is found in the *beliefs* level of culture. Beliefs are usually based on deep-seated assumptions about people and nature.

These assumptions can be justified by religious, political, and economic dogmas, and even science when used dogmatically. Being transculturally competent may require questioning these fundamental assumptions and premises, which is very difficult for most people.

An example of how beliefs influence and shape the way we do things comes from the land-ownership debate in Fiji. In recent decades there have been a series of political coups arising from ethnic differences in land-ownership beliefs, based on differing stakeholders' values and beliefs. We presented the following question to members of the three major ethnic groups in Fiji (Fijians, Fijian-Indians, and Westerners) during a workshop we conducted when the debate over land ownership was particularly prevalent in that country. We asked, "What is your belief regarding how land should be owned?" The responses were used to illustrate the different groups' values related to land ownership.

1. "Land should be owned by individuals who have the money to purchase it."
2. "Land should be owned by families and generations, and not be able to be bought and sold."
3. "The government should own all land."
4. "Humans and land are a part of nature and we really cannot own it."

Fijian villagers, because of their values for traditional collective-land tenure, tended to choose Responses 2 and 4. Westerners, whose values focus on individual ownership of land, were most likely to choose Response 1, while Fijian-Indians tended to choose Responses 1 and 3. Westerners and Fijian-Indians are relatively close in sharing individualist values related to land ownership, whereas Fijian villagers hold collectivist values. For a Westerner, ownership of land is implicitly assumed, whereas, for a Fijian villager, owning land may be as foreign to them as owning the air they breathe.

Another illustration of different values involves work incentives. A group incentive system would not be particularly attractive to most Westerners, who are accustomed to individual rewards for their efforts. Further, a Western leader who tried to implement an individual incentive program within a Fijian workplace would probably demotivate traditional Fijian workers, while motivating many Fijian-Indians. Such opposing values involving work incentives and reward systems exist in almost every nation. The following case illustrates that the way work is organized and how workers are compensated may also be a source of cultural differences.

CASE ANALYSIS: THE EXPATRIATE MANAGER AND THE VILLAGE CHIEF

We conducted training workshops for forestry managers in the South Pacific. During one of the workshops, a European expatriate who was recently hired to manage a forestry operation in Fiji expressed frustrations. He was quite vocal in expressing his difficulty with the "work ethics" of Fijian villagers. During the course of the day, his story became clearer to us. In his first week in Fiji, he asked a local village chief to send "three men to do an eight-hour job of clearing a field." Each of the three men was to be paid an hourly wage. Early the next morning, the entire group of able-bodied men from the village showed up to do the work. The expatriate, reasoning that he didn't need the 40 of them, explained to us, "I asked the group to select three men to do the work; then I asked the rest to go back to the village."

The chief responded that if all 40 men cleared the field, they could complete the work within 1 or 2 hours, then go back to the village to do other work. Further, the chief requested that the men not be paid individually. He explained to the expatriate that he would take the money for all of the workers and put it into the village fund, a traditional communal means for equally distributing money.

We asked the expatriate what his response had been. He proudly told us that he sent the chief and villagers away, only to pay higher wages to three Fijian-Indian contract workers he had transported from a nearby city. The prospect of 40 men doing the work in 1 or 2 hours, instead of three men working an 8-hour day, had perplexed him. He also did not understand the purpose of the village fund. He summarized his story by commenting on the work ethic of Fijians, saying, "They are not motivated to be productive; they just don't seem to have any individual initiative!"

We later discovered that the expatriate left his assignment after 6 months to return to England. It turned out that the village actually owned the land that the expatriate's company was using to operate their forestry business. The chief and the villagers held the ultimate control of the forestry resources on the land. In the months that followed the clearing-the-field incident, the chief and the villagers became increasingly uncooperative. This expatriate did not understand how his own Western cultural assumptions, such as his values for work performed and paid for individually rather than collectively, got in his way. In addition, he felt justified in denigrating the indigenous Fijians for their supposed lack of work ethics because of his cultural blinders. The single most important prerequisite for developing transcultural competence is to recognize that all humans come from a culture and that cultural reality has shaped every aspect of their being. There is no escaping this fact any more than one can escape from gravity.

4

Respecting Cultural Differences

Once cultural differences are recognized, the next step is to respect those differences. If the cultural prerequisites are essential aspects for understanding and managing culture, then respect for other cultures is easier to achieve. Without the other prerequisites (cultural relativity, holism, and synchronic and diachronic perspectives), respecting other cultures is not always possible. Failure to respect the cultures of others can lead to more than just a faux pas, as it can impact the ability of professionals to be able to reconcile and realize cultural dilemmas.

A LABOR STRIKE AT THE GOLD MINE

Glover was asked to consult with the owners of a Pacific Island gold mine that had recently changed ownership. The new owners were concerned when they discovered that the workers at the mine were on strike. Further,

http://dx.doi.org/10.1037/14596-004
Transcultural Competence: Navigating Cultural Differences in the Global Community, by J. Glover and H. L. Friedman

the developing nation's newly formed government was applying pressure on the mine's new general manager, who had been brought to the mine by its owners to change its "long-standing Neocolonial management and operating practices." Those practices had been symbolic of the way things had been done during the time of the previous owners and management. The strike was the legacy of the previous owners and managers.

Further, there were three distinct ethnic groups involved in the mine. The native group was composed of Pacific Islanders, a second group consisted of Indians (primarily Hindus) brought to the island by the British to work in the mine during the Colonial era, and the "Europeans" were the third group involved. The Europeans actually consisted of expatriate South African, Australian, and British mining engineers and technicians of European descent, who occupied many professional and management positions in the company.

The strikers were mostly local Pacific Islanders, who voiced many complaints. They complained that the mining company had not promoted the "right" people into the "native management training program," which had been instituted in response to a claim by the new government that too many expatriates were in the management group. They also complained that the Indian workers had been given all the "good" jobs, such as in accounting, purchasing, and other above-ground locations, while the Pacific Islanders had been assigned to the below-ground and less-desirable jobs.

Expatriates were perceived as not respecting the traditions and culture of the country in which they were working. They would swear and yell at workers, a practice in which they lost the workers' respect. They had favorites in the workforce, those who were often the younger, less traditional Pacific Islanders.

Pacific Islanders were not given time off to attend ceremonies in the villages, showing disrespect for their traditions. They complained that the expatriates did not understand the strong obligations they had to their communities. The expatriates responded that company policy only permitted 1 day of leave for weddings, funerals, and other "religious" holidays. Workers who violated the company policy were fired.

Many of the supervisors selected from the Pacific Islanders did not have the status in the traditional culture to be supervisors. The young supervisors would often be required to give orders in the workplace to chiefs and other high-ranking people from the villages.

The new owners were given an ultimatum by the island's national government: "Change the difficult situation at the mine or leave the country." Leaving would have involved turning over the management of the mine to the government and would have been very costly for the new owners. They had inherited quite a problem.

When Glover arrived as a consultant at the mine, he discovered that the traditional chiefs would not come to the mine offices to meet with the expatriate executives. Thus, no communication and negotiation was taking place. There was an uneasy standoff between the corporate leaders and the village leaders. Glover arranged to go to the villages and meet with the chiefs on their own ground, something the corporate leaders had not done.

Kava (a plant-based drink that has mild psychoactive properties) ceremonies are a fundamental practice in traditional village life throughout many of the Pacific Islands, and involve hosts offering kava to visitors. Participating in a kava ceremony demonstrates respect for tradition and also provides a means for communication with village chiefs. The failure of the mining executives to participate in the sharing of kava with the chiefs had added to the existing friction in the labor–management relationships. After participating with the chiefs in a traditional kava ceremony in the village, Glover reported to the corporate executives that the chiefs might expect the executives to also participate in such a ceremony. However, before the executives could decide if they would do so, the chiefs came into the corporate office to talk with the executives. Glover's initial show of respect brought the chiefs to the mine to begin talks. It represented the first step needed to getting a process of reconciliation and realization of the many cultural dilemmas that existed in the gold mine moving forward. Being willing to meet with the villagers and chiefs in the kava ceremony demonstrated recognition and respect for the culture of the local villagers, paving the way for reconciliation and realization. When Glover left the offices of the expatriate executive and went to the village to meet with the chiefs on their terms, he was able to demonstrate that he recognized and respected the way things were done in that country, and particularly in the villages.

SOCIOCULTURAL ENCOUNTERS, CULTURAL DILEMMAS, AND CULTURAL-VALUES DIMENSIONS

Models and methods for recognizing and respecting culture in a general way must be appropriate for any specific situation, yet have relevance across all of humanity. Again, that humans need to eat is universal, but all the other details about eating are culturally variable. To effectively accomplish this balance of general and specific, we employ an approach that enables us to operationalize the concept universally, but apply it locally. Once again, our approach uses: (1) SCEs, (2) cultural-values dimensions, and (3) cultural dilemmas to make culture operational in any given context. No matter where, there will always be actors operating in SCEs, influenced by their cultural values and often facing dilemmas of seemingly opposing differences.

There are situations, no matter what the cultural context, in which humans respond to similar needs. For example, almost every human participates in meetings of some sort. However, despite familiarity with meetings in general, there is a need for transcultural competence in meetings across many different SCEs around the globe. Going to meetings in which there are actors and stakeholders with cultural values and expectations different from one's own is fundamental to working beyond cultural boundaries. While it may be more obvious that cultural differences exist in international settings, significant cultural differences may also be found in domestic meetings within nations containing great cultural diversity, such as the United States.

Meetings may involve actors who are relatively homogeneous in cultural orientations, or the actors may be more heterogeneous in cultural orientations. The need for transcultural competence becomes more important in heterogeneous meetings, as diversity of cultural orientations creates different expectations and agendas among the meeting participants. There are many other examples of these human responses to universal needs. Negotiations, resolving conflicts, eating, hospitality to strangers, motivation of workers, and establishing agreements are just a few areas in which it is possible to observe how people with differing cultural values might respond.

Learning about culture is fundamental to transcultural competence. Learning details about a specific culture is worthwhile, but one can never anticipate all of the possible cultural variations that might be encountered. However, understanding the prerequisites of cultural relativity, synchronic and diachronic perspectives, holism, and cultural-values dimensions, as well as the 4Rs, is important for developing professionally adaptive responses within any culturally diverse SCE.

Sociocultural Encounters

An SCE may occur in any location in which there are social actors meeting with other social actors. Each SCE has a context, stakeholders with their cultural orientations, and the potential for generating cultural dilemmas. Combined with cultural dimensions and cultural dilemmas, this provides our way toward establishing a globally relevant foundation for transcultural understandings and applications, such as assessment and training.

Our focus is not just on individuals as actors as much as it is on the SCEs themselves, which always involve at least two actors. It is the pattern between the two, or among larger numbers, that determines whether SCEs are adaptive or not, as this depends not solely on the attributes of individuals but also on their interactions, which may be more than the sum of their parts. This is an important shift from the prevailing interest in individuals within a predominantly individualistic culture, as is the contemporary West. It also allows our approach to be studied scientifically through direct observations of SCEs, as opposed to asking actors to self-report about cultural variables with all of the difficulties that entails. All human interactions, including cross- and multicultural interactions, take place within an SCE.

In early human societies, most actors entered SCEs with homogeneous or at least similar worldviews, beliefs, and values. A fundamental social basis of band and tribal societies was the shared culture among the members of those societies. Conflicts and misunderstandings in SCEs due to cultural differences were infrequent, as potential misunderstandings across cultures were limited by little or no contact with others who might wander into a band or tribe's path.

As human relations evolved into more complex societies, however, their SCEs also became more complex. Trading, kinship-related village ties, population growth, and conquest of one societal group over another became more frequent reasons for humans to interact with others who were culturally different from them. Exploration, military conquest and occupation, human migration, ecological pressures, and missionary efforts were all driving forces behind increasing diversity in SCEs. Homogeneous SCEs within small cohesive groups were due to shared ethnicity, political affiliations, and economic exchange principles. However, heterogeneous SCEs became more frequent with greater diversity, and the actors within SCEs increasingly needed to understand and be competent with humans from other groups. In the era of colonialism, a common strategy for dealing with people who were culturally different involved coercion, such as using force to enslave or kill those who were different. Resource competition, distribution of power, and a complex division of labor frequently were influences related to justifications of these harsh approaches to cultural differences. In our contemporary global community, the need to find ways to reconcile cultural differences has become a major issue in many professions and cultural institutions. Businesses, governments, health and human services, education, and the military, as well as many others, are attempting to find ways to develop professions and organizations that appreciate the need to recognize cultural differences.

Cultural Dilemmas

Cultural dilemmas occur during SCEs. These dilemmas involve cultural differences that are often not well understood by the actors involved, who may approach the dilemma from their cultural vantage while being relatively blind to cultural differences in the SCE. SCEs are fundamental to understanding culture, but it is the concept of cultural dilemmas that holds the real power during SCEs. The outcome of SCEs in which cultural dilemmas need to be handled provides our way to approach transcultural competence operationally. When cultural dilemmas are handled successfully, this reflects high transcultural competence in a particular context.

Our approach is culturally relative in that there are no absolutely right or wrong ways to demonstrate transcultural competence, only relative ways dependent on cultural context. There are adaptive behaviors that work within the SCE and involve interactional, not just individual, attributes. Cultural dilemmas can be observed in SCEs within any operational context as the individual actors attempt to navigate complex, and often competing or even conflicting, circumstances. Transcultural competence in resolving and reconciling cultural dilemmas within SCEs is a fundamental professional need in culturally diverse situations.

Cultural-Values Dimensions

We use Trompenaars's cultural-dimensions model as our framework for understanding and managing culture (Trompenaars, 2012; Hampden-Turner & Trompenaars, 1993; Trompenaars & Hampden-Turner, 2002). He developed this framework more than two decades ago, and has now obtained a database of over 90,000 questionnaire responses from 52 countries to support it. Trompenaars showed how culture presents itself on different levels. At the highest level, there is the culture of a national or regional society, such as the French or West European versus the Singaporean or Oriental. At an intermediate level, the way in which culture is expressed within specific organizations can be seen as a type of culture, such as corporate culture. Finally, there is the culture of particular functions within organizations, such as marketing, research and development, and personnel departments. People within certain functional areas tend to share certain professional and ethical orientations that can be seen as a culture. For example, in the case "Does Your Vision Match Reality?" in Chapter 2, we discussed how both accounting and sales-marketing departments were more similar to each other across two organizations than they were to other departments within their own organization.

Trompenaars demonstrated that organizations can be the same in such objective dimensions as physical plant, layout, or product, yet totally different in the meanings that the surrounding human cultures read into them. He also presented the solutions to three universal problems that face mankind and distinguish cultures from each other. The problems—people's relationship to time, nature, and other human beings—are shared by humankind, but their solutions are not. The latter depends on the cultural background of the group concerned. The dimensions are based on opposites, cultural-design orientations that represent the polar extremes of how they might interact with others. In Trompenaars's approach, there are five dimensions in dealing with *relationships among people.* Universal–particular, individual–collective, achievement–ascription, specific–diffuse, and neutral–affective dimensions define the way people with a particular cultural orientation perceive their respective social worlds. *Relationships with the environment* are illustrated by the internal-external dimension. There are also *relationships with time* (sequential–synchronic and past–present–future), providing the full seven dimensions in Trompenaars's model.

Cultural dimensions are important for transcultural competence in that they provide a means for making culture operational through SCEs and are useful for comparing cultural differences. Perhaps the most important reason for understanding cultural dimensions, however, is what they offer to the 4Rs in terms of gaining adaptive outcomes with cultural dilemmas. We overview Trompenaars's 7D model, illustrating each dimension with examples. For those readers who wish to learn this approach in more depth, we recommend *Riding the Waves of Culture* (Trompenaars & Hampden-Turner, 2002) and *Business Across Cultures* (Trompenaars & Woolliams, 2004).

Universalism Versus Particularism

The universalist approach can be stated as, "What is good and right can be defined and always applies." As stated earlier about this value pole, rules are rules, and there are no exceptions to those rules. In particularist cultures, far greater attention is given to the obligations of relationships and unique circumstances, so rules vary based on differing circumstances. For example, instead of assuming that the one good way must always be followed, the particularist reasoning is that friendship has special obligations and hence may come first, while less attention is given to abstract societal codes.

Consider the fictitious case of Abby, who writes a column for the local newspaper in which she critiques restaurants. Recently, her friend Mary opens her own restaurant. Abby is invited to have dinner at Mary's new restaurant. Unfortunately, the food is not very good. Abby is faced with a universal-particular dilemma as she begins to write her critique of Mary's new restaurant. If she is a universalist, Abby will write truthfully about her experience. If she is influenced by particularistic values, she will make an exception for her friend and not give the restaurant a bad review.

Individualism Versus Communalism

Do people regard themselves primarily as individuals or primarily as part of a group? Furthermore, is it more important to focus on individual needs so that they can contribute to the collective if they wish, or is it more important to consider the collective first, since that is shared by many individuals? What is the motivator, self or society?

For example, Lester Thurow (1992) described the influence of national cultures on economic models in an article titled "Who Owns the Twenty First Century?" He presented two contemporary versions of capitalism that are operating in today's global economy—the more individualistic British-American form and the more communal German and Japanese versions. He stated:

> America and Britain trumpet individual values: the brilliant entre-preneur, Nobel prize winners, large wage differentials, individual responsibility for skills, ease of firing and quitting, profit maximiza-tion, and hostile mergers and takeovers. Germany and Japan trum-pet communitarian values: business groups, social responsibility for skills, teamwork, firm loyalty, industry strategies, and active growth-promoting industrial policies. Anglo-Saxon firms are profit maxi-mizers; Japanese firms play a game that might better be known as "strategic conquest"—they are more focused on market share than on profit. These different versions of capitalism have profound effects on everything from labor relationships to public education. (p. 50)

Thurow did not claim that the individual model of capitalism is wrong. He did, however, state that there is more to human nature than individual-ism and the desire for consumption and leisure. He also stated that humans are social builders who can work together for more collective goals.

Neutral Versus Affective

Should the nature of our interactions be objective and detached, or is expressing emotion acceptable? In North America and northwest Europe, business relationships are typically based on controlled emotions. The Western business executive has been conditioned by culture to check emotions because these are believed to confuse issues. But in other cultures, business is a human affair and the whole gamut of emotions is deemed appropriate. Loud laughter, banging your fist on the table, or leaving a meeting in anger are all part of business.

Consider the actual case of the U.S. Navy commander and the French police chief, which was told to us during research with U.S. military personnel. The commander's ship docked in Marseilles, France, for a week of shore leave. He was assigned to work with the local French police force. The initial meeting of the commander and the police chief began awkwardly. As both the French police force and the commander's crew watched, the two leaders greeted one another in the police department office. The Frenchman moved to embrace the commander, then to kiss him on both cheeks. The commander, startled by this close encounter, stepped back and offered his right hand to the police chief. The Frenchman appeared insulted by the commander's rejection of his customary French greeting. At this point, what should the American commander have done to overcome this faux pas?

- Extend his hand again to the Frenchman. Kissing and an embrace are not appropriate means for greeting (neutral values).
- Make the effort to do things the French way. Offer to embrace and allow the Frenchman to kiss both cheeks (affective values).

This case illustrates cultural differences in the way people express emotions and relate physically to one another. The cultural cues often signal respect or lack of respect for another person's culture.

Specific Versus Diffuse

When the whole person is involved in a business relationship, there is a real and personal contact, instead of only the specific relationship prescribed

by a contract. In many countries a diffuse relationship is not only preferred but is also necessary before business can proceed. A specific relationship is involved only with the issues or topics to be discussed, while a
diffuse relationship is wider and involves the actors getting to know one
another in other areas, such as family or leisure activities.

We were told about a sales representative from the United States who
was meeting with an Italian distributor. They were having an initial lunch
meeting at an upscale restaurant in Rome. The Italian began the meeting
by asking about the American's family. The American briefly responded
to his questions and then asked that they get to business by discussing the
product line he was there to sell. Undaunted by the directness of the salesman, the Italian asked if he had had time to visit some of the museums
and historical sites in Italy. Once again, the salesman dismissed that line of
conversation and opened the sales catalog to discuss the product line. This
SCE demonstrates a dilemma involving the specific values of the salesman
in seeming opposition with the Italian's desire to have a diffuse relationship in the meeting.

Achievement Versus Ascription

Achievement means that people are judged on what they have accomplished
and on their past record. *Ascription* means that status is attributed to people
through birth, kinship, position, gender, or age, as well as by connections
(who they know) and educational record (Tokyo University, an Ivy League
university, or Haute Ecole Polytechnique). For example, in an achievement
culture the question is likely to be, "What did you study?" In an ascriptive
culture, someone would probably be asked, "Where did you study?"

In research with U.S. soldiers, we were told of a case involving gender status that illustrates this dimension. A squad of four males and one
female were on a mission that required them to meet with a group of
village elders in a remote area. As they were waiting for permission from
the elders and the mayor to enter the village for the meeting, they were
told by their interpreter that the elders did not want the female (a lieu-
tenant) member of the squad to be in the meeting. The meeting was very
important to the mission. The soldiers discussed what their response

should be. Their dilemma was to respond according to their values or to operate according to the elders' values, which did not respect the female officer's status.

- The soldiers could send the message to the elders that the female officer is a member of the team and the squad will not meet with them unless she is also present (achieved values).
- Or they could ask the female officer to wait outside the village while the male members of the team meet with the elders, as the mission is too important to risk alienation of the local leaders (ascribed values).

This is just one case of many possible ways in which status is given in various cultures. When entering another culture, it is often necessary to remember that the status given back home may not be recognized in the new sociocultural context.

Relationship to Time

How people deal with time includes two aspects: how time affects ways for approaching activities and whether tradition or the future is used as a reference point. Orientation to time can affect many aspects of people's lives, from how they work to how they deal with change.

Orientation to Past, Present, and Future. People with different cultural orientations may be more or less attracted to the past, present, or future. Some live entirely in the present, or try to. Some recall the past and try to recreate it in the present. Others believe that they must focus on the future and control their own destiny. A common dilemma in change initiatives is that the change leaders may believe that previous ways of doing things need to be replaced before the new ways can be implemented.

Sequentially and Synchronically Organized Activities. There are two images that can be extracted from the concept of time. Time can be conceived as a line of sequential events passing at regular intervals. Or it can be conceived of as cyclical and repetitive, compressing past, present, and future by what these have in common: seasons and rhythms.

Confucius Versus Lewin. The ideas of Kurt Lewin (1947) are well known among change professionals in Western nations. His "unfreeze–

refreeze" model of change dynamics can be found in almost every discussion of change processes. Lewin proposed a sequential model for explaining how change might occur. He saw change as the movement through linear stages, that is, from State A to State B. An organization in State A would need to unfreeze its culture and traditional ways to implement a change initiative. Then that organization would refreeze into State B. This sequential process is compatible with the values of most Western nations, and has been the model used by most leaders in both Western and non-Western nations.

However, Robert Marshak (1993) explained that change could be viewed differently from Lewin's (1947) sequential model. There is also a synchronic model for change, based on Confucius' teachings, which has also had an important influence on how certain stakeholders, particularly those from Asian nations, might view change processes. The Confucian model of change is synchronic and cyclical in its process. Going from A to B may not be the best way to implement change in contexts where the stakeholders view the world in sequential terms. This synchronic way to see change and its processes is also commonly held by many Pacific Islanders, with whom we have worked extensively. For example, in many of these cultural contexts, it would be very inappropriate for a leader to go to workers directly to explain a planned change initiative. Instead, with Pacific Island cultures, the appropriate path would be to discuss the change with traditional ascribed leaders, gaining their approval and support first. The buy-in of those ascribed leaders would then legitimize the change initiative in the eyes of the intended recipient stakeholders. The more direct and linear approach of Westerners might offend the cultural harmony and the social dynamics of stakeholders in organization in these cultures.

Internal–External (Relationship to the Environment)

Some people are *inner directed*, seeing the major control of their lives as residing within the person. Motivations and values are derived from within. Internal values influence people to believe they can control the world around them. Other people and cultures see the world and nature as more powerful than individuals, exhibiting *outer directedness.* This orientation to the environment views humans as part of the environment and controlled by forces beyond their immediate power and influence.

Pollute or Not? While working on a development project near a village in an Asian nation, a male government contractor we knew was approached by a female NGO official. She protested that the airstrip the team was building was destroying the local fresh water supply. She showed evidence that chemicals and pollution from the construction work were contaminating the wells nearby. The contractor had been told by a commanding officer of the base that this airstrip was vital to getting supplies into the troops stationed in the region. The contractor had two options:

- Delay the project until he could resolve the pollution issue (external values).
- Go ahead with the project, ignoring the pollution issue (internal values).

The choice selected likely depends on the contractor's cultural values. If he values the environment, he is more likely to delay the project. If he feels he can control the environment, he will probably go ahead with the project.

Cultural values form the framework for understanding and applying culture. Figure 4.1 shows the model that includes the cultural dimensions discussed. In this figure, we include two additional dimensions discussed by Hofstede (2005): the dimensions of risk avoidance and power distance. These dimensions can also be used to explain cultural differences in SCEs.

CASE ANALYSIS: THE COLONEL IN JAPAN

Loy Weston is one successful change leader who did not fall into ethnocentric cultural traps when he found himself immersed in a sociocultural environment very different from the one with which he had previously been accustomed. When Kentucky Fried Chicken (KFC) hired Weston in the late 1970s to establish a fast-food franchise subsidiary in Japan, KFC headquarters in the United States and its Japanese partner, Mitsubishi Corporation, had very different ideas about how to build the business in Japan. Cultural values in the United States and Japan were opposed in

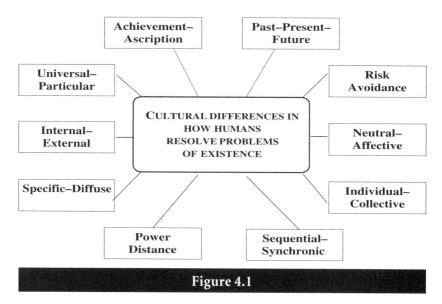

Figure 4.1

Values dimensions common to all human organizations.

many instances. In order to create a successful business venture, Weston had to design and create a management system and organizational culture that respected and eventually reconciled the opposing values of Mitsubishi and KFC. Weston's transcultural competence as a leader was the key to his success.

One of the first dilemmas Weston faced was the store design expected by KFC headquarters. Senior management required replicating the U.S. store design in Japan, but space limitations in Tokyo did not permit large buildings. Squeezing the larger store into the smaller, more cramped spaces available in Tokyo led to cost overruns and "wasted" space. Weston adapted the KFC headquarters' design for stores to fit the particular locations in Tokyo. Instead of forcing the U.S. design for a store into a Tokyo environment where it did not fit, Weston created KFC stores that fit the Tokyo environment.

In addition, KFC's menu was not always ideal for Japanese tastes. The headquarters in Louisville had very strict universal product specifications for all of its restaurants, regardless of location, but Japanese consumers did not care for mashed potatoes or coleslaw. Weston changed the menu to suit Japanese consumers, in spite of pressure from the U.S. office to maintain the same menus in Japan as were being used in the West.

Another issue Weston faced was how to advertise KFC's food in Japan. In the United States, KFC's marketing theme was that it offered consumers "good food." However, market research indicated that KFC should be positioned as "fine and elegant food" in Japan. Weston deferred to the advice of his Japanese market researchers.

Weston also had to decide whether to focus on market share or immediate profits. KFC headquarters in the United States did not share the Japanese philosophy for building market share over immediate profits. When Weston sent a financial status report to the home office, he was not able to use "building market share" as an excuse for low net earnings. Yet, the Japanese owners expected the focus to be on market-share development and reassured Weston that it was all right, and even expected, for a company to experience subpar financial performance while building market share.

The Japanese partners also expected major investments to develop KFC's workforce. Workers in Japan expected long-term, if not lifetime, employment. They expected the company to invest in their training and saw themselves as part of a group that was focused on the processes of providing a quality product to customers.

Workers in KFC stores in the United States, on the contrary, were usually students or less educated and transient employees. KFC headquarters was quick to point out that labor costs must be kept under strict control if the business were to be profitable. Job tasks were well defined by headquarters so that it was easy to replace one transient, poorly educated worker with another. Weston invested in the Japanese workers despite this being contrary to the philosophy of KFC's U.S. headquarters.

Weston is an example of a transculturally competent executive who reconciled the dilemmas of his headquarters' universalistic plan with the particularistic needs of a Japanese and United States' joint venture. Not only did he survive these early dilemmas by finding reconciled solutions, he realized them by building one of the most successful restaurant franchise businesses in history. KFC—Japan developed into 800 stores in the 10 years Weston was there, and became very profitable.

In creating KFC—Japan, Weston encountered a number of organizational and management practices that required respect for the Japanese culture and their way of doing business. The cultural values of the Japanese business environment challenged all his previously held notions of how to take care of accounting, daily operations, marketing, human resources, and business development. Weston took the strengths of both the American and Japanese business cultures and created an adaptive corporation—one that bridged the cultural gaps between the two international partners. This success in Japan led to the further expansion of KFC into the Asian market. It became the first Western restaurant chain to enter the huge Chinese market, where it is the largest fast-food operation, with more than 6,000 outlets, and it is now rapidly entering the nearly as huge Indian market. KFC has become a widely recognized symbol of Western culture for the Chinese, while in Japan "Thanksgiving" is celebrated with a "traditional" elegant meal from KFC.

Weston's ability to keep diverse stakeholders satisfied was part of his transcultural competence as a leader. There were many stakeholders in the development of KFC—Japan besides the two partner companies, KFC and Mitsubishi. These included customers, other businesses in the neighborhood where a KFC store was to open, Japanese franchisees, and the new managers and employees. Weston recognized the importance of respecting and relating to all of their cultural orientations. He was also able to reconcile and realize cultural differences between his home office in the United States and his operation in Japan. Unfortunately, Weston was an exception to the norm. We have observed many more cases of transculturally incompetent professionals than we have of transculturally competent professionals.

5

Reconciling Cultural Differences

In the *The Crack Up*, F. Scott Fitzgerald (1945) stated, "The test of a first-rate intelligence is the ability to hold two opposed ideas in the mind at the same time, and still retain the ability to function" (p. 69). We start with that well-known quote because it illustrates the paradoxical nature of the cultural-dilemma process, holding opposites to the point where they might be represented as complements, two sides of the same coin. Transculturally competent professionals need to do more than be able to cope with cultural differences; they need to create a synergy that reconciles dilemmas in new ways.

Change requires innovation, coming up with something new. Whether it involves a new technology, marketing policy, project portfolio, or service schedule externally, or a new way of understanding and even valuing internally, once change is implemented things are no longer the same and have moved into a new phase of existence. Transcultural competence

http://dx.doi.org/10.1037/14596-005
Transcultural Competence: Navigating Cultural Differences in the Global Community, by J. Glover and H. L. Friedman

requires reconciling cultural dilemmas and being innovative in appropriate and creative ways.

Cultural diversity, combined with changes created by rapidly evolving technological, political, and economic climates, has created many dilemmas and challenges globally and locally. It has become increasingly obvious that the world is very diverse, populated by many groups of people with different ways of understanding and doing things. Professionals must be able to interact with a variety of people who do not always share their way of seeing the world or their view of how to organize and manage their professional work. Being able to reconcile and realize appropriate solutions to cultural differences is essential to being transculturally competent.

We refer to this innovative process as "creating new boxes." A new box is essentially a new way to do things. It results from what previously was a cultural dilemma with seemingly opposing values. We stress using the term "new boxes" because thinking from "outside the box" does not change the box, even though you may be thinking differently from the past. You are still looking at the same box.

The appropriateness and effectiveness of any innovative strategy depend necessarily on cultural and environmental context and not just on an individual's knowledge, skills, and abilities. Instead, appropriateness and effectiveness rely on an adaptive match. Successful change depends more on matching the change strategy with the cultural expectations of stakeholders than it does on any best practices. In some cultural contexts, people may be accustomed to autocratic change initiatives. In other cultural contexts, they may want consensus and participation in the change process. Transcultural competence involves sensing and responding to this match, being attuned to the relationship between individual and/or organization and its context.

THE TYRANNY OF THE OR AND THE GENIUS OF THE AND

In change and development initiatives, an underlying assumption often held by change leaders is that a new way of doing things must replace the previous way. Those favoring the new ways may discredit the past and those people who value the past. To implement this, the leader rids the organization of that!

But successful change and innovation are rarely created by arbitrarily replacing old ways with new ones. In some instances, a stakeholder may advocate for a particular way to do things over someone else's way. As an example, there can be a struggle between headquarters and a local field office regarding policies or reporting systems. Both sides may feel that its position is the one best way. Change initiatives implemented in this manner often result in a lose–lose or, at best a win–lose, result for most stakeholders.

It seems that leaders are always faced with choices between the past and the future, this or that approach to a situation, and following one model versus another. Collins and Porras (1994) referred to this leadership problem as the "tyranny of the OR." The OR view does not accept paradox, and it cannot live with two seemingly contradictory forces or ideas at the same time. The OR pushes people to believe that things must be one way OR another, but not both.

For example, leaders may be controlled by mind-sets that expect change OR stability, low cost OR high quality, investing in the future OR doing well in the short term, creating wealth for shareholders OR doing good in the world. The OR becomes a way of perceiving reality that often prevents adaptive responses from leaders who hold those perceptions. It acts as a cultural trap, limiting the ability to see alternatives that might be better than what is held as truth.

Collins and Porras (1994) pointed out the yin/yang concept of Chinese dualistic philosophy as an alternative to the either/or way of thinking. They described the process of seeing opposites as complementary, not contradictory, as the "genius of the AND." The genius of the AND consists of the ability to embrace both extremes of a dimension at the same time. Instead of choosing between A and B, leaders who follow the yin/yang philosophy figure out a way to have both A AND B. Long term AND short term, profits AND good for the world, low costs AND quality are all possible if the OR can be replaced with the AND.

Periods of change in organizations need not be traumatic and uncertain. Change initiatives can give the security and familiarity of past behaviors AND the advantages of the new ways found in the change initiative. In economic and community development situations, what would be the adaptive advantage if leaders could preserve the best of traditional organizational culture, while implementing a change initiative that adds value to existing cultural orientations? In corporate change initiatives, how much more effective would change initiatives be if stakeholders' values could be reconciled in the design?

The AND is more than just a combination of existing parts or elements. It does not represent balance such as might be observed in a compromise. Yin and yang are not a blend that is neither highly yin nor highly yang. Instead, the combination aims to be distinctly yin AND distinctly yang—at the same time, all the time. In more Western terms, value is added to the existing way of doing things. The innovation that is to be implemented represents a breaking out of existing mind-sets and creation of a new cultural orientation built of the combined strengths of what went before.

Transcultural competence requires facing dilemmas through creative change solutions. For example, how can an organization cut costs and still remain customer focused? Can the environment be protected and profits still be made? Can workers be empowered and appropriate controls maintained? Is it possible to implement technological improvements such as automated answering systems and maintain high levels of customer satisfaction? How can teams and individuals be rewarded in the same workplace? How can downsizing be done while keeping employee loyalty? To avoid the tyranny of the OR, one needs to question fundamental premises regarding managing, organizations, and change. This relates to avoiding cultural traps, as well as to reconciling and realizing good solutions, which are all part of transcultural competence.

CASE ANALYSIS: BLUE HORIZON CRUISES

Blue Horizon Cruises is a fictional cruise ship company somewhere in the South Pacific. This case involves a combination of situations and characters based on the consulting work that Glover conducted in the Pacific

Islands and the Caribbean. It is presented as a simulation to illustrate how the cultural-dilemmas process can operate in community and national development initiatives.

The stakeholders of Blue Horizon have a fundamental cultural dilemma: Do they ignore what caused them to be materially successful, a beautiful environment, in order to pursue even more of that success, or do they retain a sense of place with local villages and the natural environment remaining pristine at the expense of growing more material success? This case involves a rapidly growing ecotourism business in a tropical setting. Blue Horizon represents an organization whose past success created a potential cultural trap in which the very product that made them successful may cause the company's demise. Although most have never been a cruise-ship executive or a village chief, almost all can relate to their differing cultural orientations in this simulation, as nearly everyone has values regarding growth, the environment and natural resources, and the impact of change on communities.

The Setting

Blue Horizon operates a successful ecotourism business in a Pacific Island nation. The leaders built a rapidly growing business by marketing to Japanese, German, American, and Australian visitors who want to experience the "real South Pacific." Its operation is located in "Kona," a fictitious emerging nation that has made a strong effort to use tourism as a major component of its economic-development efforts, and all stakeholders are also fictional in this simulation.

The cruise trips offered by Blue Horizon visit an idyllic group of islands where travel brochures describing the physical environment conjure up visions of a pristine tropical paradise. The inhabitants of the area still live and work in a traditional manner, reminiscent of earlier times. Because of the beautiful physical setting and traditional village life, visitors have been extremely satisfied with their cruise experiences with Blue Horizon.

Blue Horizon has experienced remarkable growth and profitability in its 10-year history. Except for the first year of operation, the company has operated in the black. During the first decade of operation, the fleet had been expanded from three ships to 10 in an effort to keep up with the demand for the cruises. The company was eventually sold to a New Zealand businessperson in 1994. The new owner expected the company to continue its high financial return into the future.

Trouble in Paradise?

Despite the idyllic setting, Blue Horizon stakeholders faced four major problems that illustrate the seemingly opposing values of the company's stakeholders. Each problem included a key cultural dilemma with one or more of Trompenaars's (2012) seven cultural dimensions represented in the stakeholders' orientations. The four problems were as follows.

An environmental study indicated that the reefs in the areas visited by Blue Horizon's ships may be in danger. After several years, potential problems had begun to emerge. An environmental group conducted a study to evaluate the impact of tourism on the reefs in the area. The results suggested that unless Blue Horizon took steps to minimize their impact on the reef, considerable damage could occur in the next 5 years. This was apparently due to the fact that Blue Horizon had increased the number of cruises each week from three cruises in its first year of operation to 30 cruises 10 years later. Market projections indicated that the demand could support as many as 40 cruises per week in the near future. However, frequent anchoring by the ships was creating damage. The key dilemma was, "Do we protect the natural reefs OR do we continue with rapid tourism growth in the area?" A reconciled solution might be expected to result in both further development of tourism AND the preservation of the reef.

Tourists were complaining that the native culture may be losing its charm. The traditional customs and hospitality enjoyed by previous visitors were beginning to change. The traditional village culture had fostered genuine hospitality and generosity. However, economic development and a market economy created fewer smiles and more entrepreneurs. People in the villages were becoming more motivated by "the dollar." Several villages had developed thriving cash economies from the sale of straw goods and other tourism artifacts manufactured by local cottage industries operated by enterprising villagers. Tourists from the cruise ships had begun to complain about the commercial nature of their interactions with villagers. One unhappy visitor griped, "All they seem to care about is selling us trinkets, and we even noticed a 'made in Taiwan' sign on the base of one of the gifts we bought in a village market." The key dilemma was, "Do we continue to develop the new cash economy OR do we maintain the traditional culture and its substantive economy at all costs?" A reconciled solution might be to find ways to have the villagers realize the importance of their traditional culture, even during commercial transactions, that is, find ways to have tourism AND maintain the traditional culture.

A third problem area was the government's agenda. The government wanted to achieve maximum benefit from the Blue Horizon success. A developer was planning a small resort and golf course. As with most developing nations, the government leaders were interested in creating capital from local resources. The Kona minister for tourism development was in the process of negotiations with an American investor to finance a small luxury resort and an 18-hole golf course on one of the pristine islands. Developers argued that the resort would bring "much needed jobs to local villagers."

However, this action would have great impacts on both the natural environment and people in the area. The key dilemma was one of tradition versus growth. Were the villagers better off working in a resort as waiters and housekeepers OR should they be left to continue their subsistence economy? The resort and golf course would bring jobs in the Western sense, but the villagers had adapted for 2,000 years without them. A reconciled solution would involve a means for development AND tradition, with the past paving the way for the future.

The fourth potential problem for Blue Horizon was the eroding power of the village chiefs and elders. Many of the traditional leaders were becoming alarmed to see their ways eroding in the face of rapid development. They also sensed their political power diminishing as many younger villagers obtained wage-labor jobs and were no longer being dependent on the village fund and the communal-subsistence economy. They also felt that all income paid to villagers should be paid to the village fund, a system of redistribution and communal sharing controlled by the village chiefs. They asked Blue Horizon to not permit any cash to exchange hands between the market vendors and the visitors. Instead, the chiefs asked that all monies be collected by the ship's captain and turned over to the village chief. If Blue Horizon did not comply with the suggested distribution of tourist revenues to the villages, the chiefs had threatened to prohibit the cruise ships from visiting the villages. This was a classic dilemma of market capitalism OR traditional resource-distribution mechanisms. A reconciled solution would permit the chiefs to maintain the village fund AND the village entrepreneurs to keep a part of their earnings.

The Reconciliation Process

Given the possible difficulties that these problems might bring, the CEO and principal stock owner of Blue Horizon, Ian Thomas, asked his managing director, John McClean, to look into the matters. John McClean had worked in Kona for over 10 years and was one of the first executives hired by the original owners to develop the fledgling Blue Horizon operation. He had a deep appreciation for these islands and was very concerned about the potential dilemmas faced by the company. Both John and Ian agreed that it was time to review the operating strategy of Blue Horizon.

John contacted a consultant from Seattle who had extensive experience in troubleshooting economic development problems such as those Blue Horizon was facing. This consultant, Mary Franklin, suggested that she also involve Brian Olsen, an anthropologist and ecotourism expert from a university in Oregon. Brian and Mary arrived in Kona and arranged a meeting with the important stakeholders for Blue Horizon.

Blue Horizon's Stakeholders

The consultants' goal was to elicit the cultural dilemmas and the seemingly opposing cultural orientations held by the principal stakeholders in Blue Horizon's situation. To accomplish this, they discussed the four problems with the following stakeholders:

- Ian Thomas, CEO and principal owner. Ian is an individualist and believes in the market system. He finds some of the other stakeholders, particularly the chief and the environmentalist, to be difficult people. His cultural orientation includes universalism, individualism, achievement, specific, neutral, internal, sequential, and future cultural values.

- John McClean, managing director. John has lived in the islands for years and feels a strong identity with those who wish to preserve the reef, traditional village life, and the power of the chiefs. His cultural values include particularism, collectivism, achievement, diffuse, neutral, internal, synchronic, and present cultural values.

- Marta Tufu, minister of tourism development for Kona. Marta went to a business school in the United States and is very prodevelopment. Some locals feel Marta is more like the outsiders than her own people. Her cultural orientation includes universalism, collective, achievement, diffuse, neutral, internal, synchronic, and present cultural values.

- Tomasi Va'valu, paramount chief of the villages. Tomasi feels a responsibility to preserve the traditional ways of life in the village and also the natural environment. He resents those who are trying to change everything for their own selfish reasons. His cultural orientation includes particularism, collective, ascriptive, diffuse, neutral, external, synchronic, and past cultural values.

- Joan Collins, representative of the World Watch Environmental Protection organization. Joan commissioned a study that clearly showed the damage Blue Horizon is doing to the reef. She finds Ian to be a callous businessman who does not care about the islands and their people. Her cultural orientation includes particularism, collectivism, ascriptive, diffuse, neutral, external, sequential, and present cultural values.

- Joni Keritu, self-appointed representative of the villager vendors. Joni has developed a business selling trinkets to tourists from the cruise ships who visit the villages. He thinks the chief should not have a say in keeping development from happening. His cultural orientation includes universalism, individualism, achievement, diffuse, neutral, internal, sequential, and present cultural values.

Following the initial meeting, the two consultants planned to lead a second meeting in which the stakeholders use a four-step approach for dilemma reconciliation. The deliverable result of the meeting was expected to be the reconciled solution, or a new box, for each of the four problems. The new box was expected to incorporate the strengths of the existing stakeholders' cultural orientations, while minimizing their weaknesses. Realizing and making the solution a reality, which involves implementing the new box so that it will be accepted by the various stakeholders, is to be addressed at future meetings.

Dilemma-Reconciliation Process

Essentially, this dilemma-reconciliation process involves four steps, following Trompenaars's (2012) approach. The Blue Horizon Cruises case is used to illustrate how the consultants and stakeholders might use this four-step process. For brevity, we focus primarily on the reef damage versus other dilemmas within the simulation.

Step 1: Identify the Dilemma

When we work with organizations and communities to assess and/or change culture, we begin by eliciting cultural dilemmas. This dilemma identification process may use focus groups, document analysis, participant observation, attendance in meetings, interviews, and other methods that have participants in organizations and groups identify SCEs in which there are stakeholders with seemingly opposing cultural values and orientations. As researchers and consultants, we briefly explain what a cultural dilemma is, provide examples, and then ask the participants to identify and discuss dilemmas from their actual experiences during SCEs in their organization and/or community. These dilemmas are then analyzed using Steps 2, 3, and 4.

In this simulation, the reef-damage problem had been established through the observations of stakeholders, particularly the chief and the environmentalist. The report from the environmental group added credibility to the claims of those stakeholders who felt that preservation of the reef at all costs was a priority. On the other hand, Blue Horizon Cruises' owner, investors, and the minister of tourism did not share the cultural orientations of the chiefs and environmentalists. Instead, they felt that the economic growth (perceived in market economy terms) was the highest priority in this dilemma.

Step 2: Charting the Cultural Space

After dilemmas are identified, we then select what seem to be the most important ones to chart. Charting is accomplished using a two-dimensional grid (see Figure 5.1), based on a scale of 0 to 10 on each opposing axis, used for measuring value orientations. For example, in a dilemma in which individualism–collectivism is a prominent cultural dimension, we would put individualism on one axis and collectivism on the other. The extreme high of individualism would be assigned 0, 10 and of collectivism would be assigned 10, 0. Neutral expressions, low in both individualism and collectivism, would be assigned to 0, 0 and a compromise moderate in both would be assigned 5, 5. This makes positions on a value dimension visible through the grid.

Charting dilemmas enables one to understand the "cultural space" among stakeholders. Charting also permits an understanding of the most

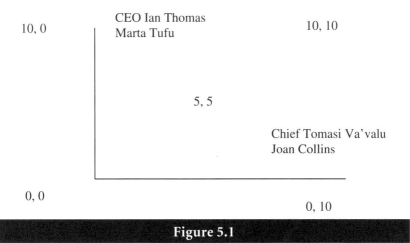

Figure 5.1

Charting cultural space.

polarized positions among stakeholders, which is often where conflicts reside. Knowing these opposite cultural orientations can lead to the analysis of the strengths and weaknesses of each position.

Stakeholder differences on the reef problem were primarily influenced by a conflict on the dimension of internal and external values. The illustration in Figure 5.1 places Ian, the CEO in the simulation, on the chart as a 10, 0 (with this representing maximum external cultural values and minimal internal cultural values). Internal cultural values are based on the belief that control of the environment is possible. Tomasi, the chief in that simulation, is placed on the opposite position in the chart at 0, 10 (with this representing minimal external cultural values and maximum internal cultural values). External cultural values are based on the belief that the environment controls those who are in it.

These are polar-opposite positions on the reef issue, which can be easily seen on the grid. Other stakeholders would be charted to fall somewhere between these two extreme cultural-values positions on this dimension. Other important grid positions are 0, 0 (representing an "apathetic position" that is low on both toward the problem) and 5, 5 (representing a "compromise" position, with each side willing to give up something). In addition, there is the 10, 10 position, which is the desired reconciled solution, using the strengths of each opposite position while avoiding the weaknesses of each opposite position.

All positions, except for the 10, 10 reconciliation, are less than acceptable in creating successful change and demonstrating transcultural competence. The apathy position (0, 0) is commonly found and can, in many cases, be a "survival" strategy for a stakeholder, since they would not have to take a stand or commit to one side or the other of the dilemma. Extremes such as "my way or the highway" (10, 0 or 0, 10) seldom work when stakeholders resist change initiatives shoved down their collective throats. Even compromise (5, 5) has its difficulties, since both opposite stakeholder groups must give up something (often to get the other side to give up something) in the compromise process, leaving both unsatisfied.

Transculturally competent professionals strive for 10, 10 solutions, which involve creating a new box or a way of addressing the dilemma not previously in place. This reconciled position, by building on the strengths of each stakeholder position, involves innovative thinking and creating synergy from diversity as the focus of the change process. Using this grid also allows the value positions to be operationalized for purposes of scientific research and practice.

Step 3: Strengths and Weaknesses of Opposing Values

We then may use this charting of cultural space to generate discussions on the strengths and weaknesses of each opposite stakeholders' cultural values position. This discussion identifies a starting point for creating a new way to respond to the SCE and the stakeholders' differences. For example, if the dilemma involves the reef damage, we can list the strengths of the external-values approach (CEO's), while also listing its weaknesses. Then, we can list the strengths of the internal approaches (chief's), while also listing the weaknesses. It is also very important to consider the SCE as a context and recognize when the environment surrounding the dilemma may have relevance to the stakeholders. What initially might have been viewed as irreconcilably opposite-value positions can often be seen more clearly through this process, enabling a values change toward reconciliation, which often can be seen on the grid as a shift toward a 10, 10 location, as initially oppositional stakeholders might come to see the benefits of being high on both sides of the dilemma. Table 5.1 shows a way to identify the strengths and weaknesses of opposites.

Step 4: Creating New Boxes for Human Interaction

We use the term "new box" to refer to a reconciled solution to a dilemma. We use new box because thinking "outside the box" is not enough, as the box creating the dilemma is still there. The old box is still the way to do things. A new box is a creative design for doing things differently from what was done before the dilemma was identified. Reconciliation is a form of cultural innovation, and reconciled solutions are found by taking the strengths of opposite stakeholder positions while minimizing their weaknesses. For the reconciliation of the reef damage versus stopping the cruise ship expansion, Table 5.2 provides some possible solutions for creating the new box.

Table 5.1

Stated Positions for Reef-Damage Reconciliation

Stakeholder	Cultural orientations	Stated positions	Strengths	Weaknesses
Ian Thomas, CEO	Internal	Continue cruise-ship operations	Immediate prosperity for some stakeholders	Long-term damage to the tourism product
Chief Tomasi Va'valu	External	Stop the cruise-ship operations	Preservation of natural resource— the reef	Village market economy would decline

Table 5.2

Creative Solutions for Problem One (Reef Damage)

Proposed Solutions	How Does This Solution Demonstrate "The Genius of the AND?"	Implement?
Install mooring buoys to avoid the ships having to use anchors in the reef areas.	Cruise ships can continue to visit the reef and the village AND the reef damage from ship anchors can be minimized or avoided entirely.	YES
Under the direction of the chiefs, develop a ferry service from the cruise ships to the shore/villages. Use local outrigger canoes or small boats owned by the villagers.	Cruise ships need not come inside the reef to access the villages AND local-village market economy is supported AND traditional political power of chiefs is recognized.	YES
A pier is constructed to extend over the reef and permit the cruise ships to dock outside the reef.	Costly solution that will create more reef damage. Solution becomes another problem. It does not demonstrate an effective application of the AND.	NO
Replace existing cruise-ship fleet with smaller craft capable of coming inside the reef to anchor.	Very costly solution for company. Existing cruise ships are very popular with passengers. It does not demonstrate an effective application of the AND.	NO

The preferred solutions, mooring buoys and a water taxi service operated by the chief and the villagers, were created from the strengths of both the CEO's and chief's positions. These new boxes are a new way to look at the old problem. They enable stakeholders to practice the "genius of the AND" while avoiding the "tyranny of the OR." That is what reconciling and realizing cultural dilemmas is all about.

Using this case as a training simulation, by asking trainees to role play the various stakeholders, has been helpful in our work around the world in teaching transcultural competence to consultants and other professionals. This case teaches how to recognize dilemmas on value dimensions by charting them in cultural space. Then, by discussing their strengths and weaknesses, respect for differences on these dimensions is encouraged. In working toward reconciling these differences, apathy (one or both sides passively accepting differences without any change) and compromise (each side giving up some important aspects of the differences to get along) solutions can be avoided, as can outcomes in which one side wins at the expense of the other, which loses. The creative solution of the dilemma, a new box, is possible when the new approach to the dilemma is realized.

6

Realizing Cultural Differences

Realizing the solutions needed to reconcile cultural dilemmas involves implementing the new box solution in the sociocultural context. Creating new boxes through reconciliation alone means little without realization. Reconciliation of a cultural dilemma requires creativity in problem solving, but extending what has been reconciled into a realization is the final stage of the 4Rs for dealing with cultural differences. Transcultural competence requires knowledge and of how to make change happen, and skills in doing so, so that the new-box solution will be accepted and embraced by the stakeholders. Realizing involves making the new way of handling a situation in a sociocultural encounter (SCE) that led to a dilemma solved not just in theory but in practice. Many ideas for solutions are good in theory but may fail in practice, so implementing new boxes

http://dx.doi.org/10.1037/14596-006
Transcultural Competence: Navigating Cultural Differences in the Global Community, by J. Glover and H. L. Friedman

requires more than reconciling cultural dilemmas—it also involves making the new box "stick."

Many additional dilemmas may occur in the process of attempting to realize a cultural dilemma's reconciled solution. One common additional dilemma involves time, namely, through reconciling past, present, and future perspectives. A key question is often, "How can we use the past to help us get to the future?" In contrast, when a dilemma is not properly reconciled, the question posed might instead be, "How can we forget the past so we can implement our future?" That question, however, is laden with pitfalls likely to sabotage any lasting realization. Another common question related to realization is, "How can we reconcile the universal expectations of the corporate office with the values in the local context?" Arriving at a reconciliation of this dilemma at the local level is often thwarted in its implementation at headquarters. A third common realization dilemma involves the process for implementing the new box, namely, "Will the process be linear, going from A to B, or will the process be more synchronic, perhaps going from A to C to get to B?"

ROGERS'S FIVE ATTRIBUTES OF INNOVATION

Everett Rogers (1983), in his classic research on innovation diffusion, provided five attributes of innovations that are helpful in developing the design of reconciled solutions to cultural dilemmas. It is helpful to evaluate the 10, 10 solutions to dilemmas using these five attributes.

Relative Advantage

As new boxes, or reconciled solutions, are being evaluated by potential adopters (dilemma stakeholders), they usually ask, "What's in it for me?" Stakeholders will also evaluate the new reconciled solution in terms of what risks are involved if they should choose to adopt it. Both of these decisions are included in the relative advantage attribute. If dilemma stakeholders are involved in the reconciliation process, and they feel that their cultural orientations have been recognized and respected in the process, then they will probably be more receptive to accept the solution.

Compatibility

Innovations that do not match the various stakeholders' ideas of how the world should be may be resisted or rejected. Compatibility includes being consistent with the cultural values involved in a dilemma. If the reconciled solution includes the strengths of each opposite position when the cultural space is charted, it is a good way to ensure compatibility.

Complexity

Reconciled solutions need to avoid complexity. Stakeholders may not understand complicated solutions, no matter how worthwhile they might be. For example, the mooring buoys solution in the Blue Horizon Cruises case is not complex, and all stakeholders could relate to the solution.

Trialability

Reconciled solutions should be easy to experience. If solutions are not easily available to try, stakeholders may not be willing to risk changing to fit the new box. Those professionals who create innovative and reconciled solutions need to make certain that stakeholders are able to "sample" what happens when the new solution is implemented.

Observability

Innovations are observed by potential adopters. As innovations are observed, potential adopters assess what is happening to those who are the early adopters. How did they benefit or not benefit? How did accepting the new box affect them? The next group of adopters then makes decisions as to whether or not to adopt based on what they observed with the first group.

TIME, RESOURCES, AND PRIORITIES

Fredrik Barth (1967) provided another method for enhancing the potential for a reconciled solution to be realized. He contended that change and innovation is a process that can be measured by observing how people use their time, allocate resources, and establish priorities. If there is a change in the way these three activities happen within a sociocultural context, then the process is happening. Once a dilemma is reconciled, it is possible to measure progress in realizing the dilemmas by using Barth's model. The following case illustrates how time, resources, and priorities did not change.

THE PRODUCTIVITY DILEMMA

A U.S. Navy admiral told us a story of frustration concerning his efforts to bring about a continuous improvement initiative among sailors in his command at a naval shipyard responsible for repairing and maintaining the Pacific fleet. "I don't know why nothing seems to be changing! We trained all 2,200 sailors in statistical process methods. Every person in my command completed a three-day course during the past year," he explained.

When the admiral was asked what else he had done to create cultural change, he looked somewhat befuddled and responded, "Nothing except for the training." In actuality, what he had done was train 2,200 sailors to statistically chart their dissatisfaction with their workplace. He had confused merely training the sailors in statistics with actually implementing any adaptive redesign of his organization that might have created an environment of continuous improvement.

Despite the admiral's well-intended attempts at creating a useful improvement in his organization, the culture of the naval shipyard had not changed for the better. Even though the 2,200 sailors knew how to use the concepts and methods of statistical process methods, they were unable to apply what they had learned in the workplace. Systemic blockages, arising from the old ways of doing things, were still at work. For example, those sailors who wanted to apply what they had learned to solve problems in their workplace were seldom given the time to do so. Instead, they were told to focus on their "real jobs." Furthermore, many of the noncommissioned officers were threatened by the new awareness of workplace problems and actually became more resistant to any effective change. The training had been specific in its design and application. Unfortunately, a more diffuse approach, incorporating the workplace culture, was needed. The Admiral, like so many other leaders, failed to recognize that he was dealing with organizational culture. He also did not have a means for making the culture he intended to change operational. It is essential for transculturally competent professionals to have a framework that enables them to make sense of the complexities of culture, particularly when they are attempting to create changes. We have developed such a framework to enable us to make culture operational and understood by those professionals who wish to work with cultural diversity and across cultural boundaries.

FADS AND CHANGE

In recent years it has become very popular to implement "teams" in Western organizations. Leaders have often been persuaded to create a "team culture" in their workplace in order to remain on the leading edge of management practice, regardless of whether or not this fits the overall organization culture. Unfortunately, many change projects involving the wholesale implementation of innovations fail to be realized, especially if these are motivated simply by fashion trends rather than recognition of cultural differences accompanied by respect and thoughtful reconciliation. Consequently, teams have often failed to be successfully implemented. We even know of one consultant who now specializes in "de-teaming" organizations that were forced to develop a team approach but are finding that the original culture of the organization was not adequately reconciled with the cultural design necessary for team development.

Individual versus collective values are about behaving independently or as a group. In an organization with a collective orientation, the needs of the group take priority over the needs of specific individuals. It is the opposite in organizations with individual orientations, where individual needs take priority over the group. Depending on the cultural orientation of organizational stakeholders, teams may or may not be the most effective way to organize a workplace. Also important is the specific cultural design selected for a team approach. For example, cross-functional teams imposed on a function-based organization are very difficult to implement. Such differing cultural designs require considerable prior reconciliation to avoid change failure.

RECONCILING MANAGEMENT AND LABOR PARTICIPATION IN A FACTORY

In a change project at a Latin American factory, we were asked to develop teams for improving the workplace and improving productivity. However, the general manager had concerns that the union leadership would resist the new "team approach" because they would perceive it as a management ploy, as there had been considerable management–union tension in recent months. We recommended that the manager appoint the union leaders as the leaders of the new team. It was a message from management to the union leaders that their traditional roles with employees would not be subverted by the change project. It was also an attempt to reconcile the union leaders' roles with the development of the new team approach to solving workplace problems. Although the union warmed to the idea, the managers remained uncertain and somewhat cautious. It took considerable persuasion on our part, as consultants, to get the general manager to go along with our plan.

After several meetings with the teams, it became apparent that our reconciliation approach was working, and the change was being successfully realized. Union leaders applied their traditional influence to persuade employees to adopt the new team approach. With our strategy, we had effectively neutralized the potential for resistance from union leaders, since they were the ones actually leading the new teams. Had we not included the union leaders, they most certainly would have led an organized resistance to the new idea in the workplace. Instead, they became some of the most avid supporters of the change initiative, particularly since they were given important roles to play in the new cultural design of the workplace.

In change initiatives, the helmsman of change must negotiate the "cultural space" between the old and the new, as well as other cultural oppositions. The eventual adoption of the new ways prescribed by the change initiative will be facilitated by bringing together various stakeholders to accept and follow the new cultural approach. The change method needs to focus on the means for reconciling the best of each stakeholder's cultural orientations, while minimizing weaknesses. Essentially, the new change perspective should include a consideration of the influence of the stakeholders' cultural-design orientations on the process of change.

Social changes that actually do occur should be studied in a context that considers all those that might occur. "We must look into the possibilities derived from our models, and not stop merely with what in fact has happened historically. . . . Evolution is what happens that makes it impossible to happen still another time" (Bohannan, 1995, pp. 142–43). The following case illustrates the need to understand change from a diachronic perspective.

CASE ANALYSIS: RUBBISH IN THE PARKING LOT

Glover had been asked to develop problem-solving teams for a community hospital. The facility was part of a for-profit service company that had been operating in the community for over two decades. He had met the hospital administrator, Bob Selmer (note that the names of all the stakeholders in this case are fictitious) at a conference where Bob had heard a fellow administrator speak on the benefits of employee participation in the service industries. A few days later, Bob called Glover to ask for help with a new change initiative, implementing employee problem-solving teams.

"Do you think you could help me put in a team culture at the hospital?" Bob's voice was ringing with enthusiasm. "When I heard my colleague speaking about his employee teams at the last manager's conference in Brisbane, I became convinced that I need to do something similar at my property."

"I will help you, but we need to work out an implementation plan that will work for you," Glover replied. They spoke in general terms about what Bob might expect, but Glover was aware that Bob needed more time to grasp his challenge.

They met the following week and developed their plan. Bob was clearly eager to get started and seemed willing to commit the necessary resources. However, Glover was concerned that Bob was not really aware of all the changes he would need to make to be successful with the proposed team system. There was also another complication: Bob's union employees had just come back from a long and bitter strike a few months earlier.

Glover's first step was to educate the Executive Committee and gain their involvement. Bob made his opening remarks, and then turned over the group to Glover. For the most part, Bob's managers were also enthused to try the new team approach to dealing with their employees. After a 3-day workshop, everyone left with a good impression about the future of this project.

Next, they began to form and train employee teams, which were organized by department. Maintenance and Engineering was the first team. Most of these team members were long-term employees and possessed considerable skills as electricians, plumbers, painters, landscapers, and mechanics. They considered themselves to be the department that was responsible for keeping the hospital operating. One long-term employee proudly described them as "the glue that held the hospital together." However, as they left the initial training session, Bob explained to Glover that he had been disappointed with that department since he had taken over as general manager over 2 years ago. He felt that they did not spend enough of their time doing programmed maintenance on the physical property and grounds of the hospital.

The Plot Thickens

They spent the next morning with the Maintenance and Engineering team, leading them in a process of brainstorming and priority ranking of the day-to-day problems they were facing. The group identified over 30 problems, covering a wide range of issues.

When they finished the morning session, they had ranked the number one problem as "rubbish in the car park." The entire group applauded when the team leader told them that they would give that problem their top priority.

Glover noticed Bob's body language as the group reached consensus on the rubbish problem. Bob leaned over and whispered to Glover, "There must be more important problems for Maintenance and Engineering to work on. Why not programmed maintenance?"

After considerable discussion with Glover following the meeting, Bob agreed to keep his views to himself and let the team work on the problem of their choice. But it was obvious that he was a little deflated about the whole process.

Two months passed, and the team became more and more committed to "fixing" the rubbish in the car park problem. As Glover attended their weekly meetings, he could sense that the group was developing a sense of self-determination they had not previously experienced in their workplace. As the weeks passed, they became more and more passionate about their task of resolving the rubbish problem.

History Explains It All

They interviewed people in the hospital who had been a part of the problem's history. No one seemed to know how the problem had evolved, until a department head, who had been at the property for 15 years, recalled the origin of the problem. He related the story at one of the team meetings:

> Ten years ago, a former hospital administrator had come back from a lunch meeting in town and became upset to see that the car park was littered with rubbish. He was hosting the visit of a corporate vice president later that day. Impulsively, he immediately went to his office and phoned Housekeeping. He became even more frustrated when no one in that department answered the phone. A supervisor from Maintenance and Engineering happened to walk by the hospital administrator's office. He was summoned into the office and instructed to immediately send out all of his available staff to clean up the rubbish.

And so the rubbish in the car park problem had begun. Ten years later, the whim and impulsive directive of the previous hospital administrator had become a formal part of the job duties of the Maintenance and Engineering staff. It had even been put on their job descriptions! Over the years, the staff complained to their supervisors, but nothing could remove this task from their daily duties.

The Hospital Administrator Changes His Mind

After months of participation and problem-solving exercises, the team members presented the results of their analysis to Bob at a formal meeting. The team leader described the consequences of the "rubbish" problem.

Time away from other duties was a primary concern of the team members. The team had tracked the number of staff hours spent each week cleaning rubbish in the car park. All were amazed to see that 16 staff hours were spent dealing with rubbish each week. "Sixteen staff hours times our average rate of pay, $16 per hour, equals $256 in labor costs to the hospital per week. That's roughly $13,000 per year!" The team leader clearly articulated this, glancing frequently at Bob to gauge his reaction to this news.

A second concern was the out-of-order patient rooms in the hospital. Frequently, patient rooms were taken out of service due to electrical, air conditioning, plumbing, and other areas normally repaired by Maintenance and Engineering staff. This often resulted in requested rooms not being available, newly arrived patients being moved to share rooms after finding that their room had problems, or patients being tolerant but silently vowing to never return to such a poorly maintained hospital in the future. Bob listened intently to the team leader as the presentation continued.

Moving patients to share what were meant to be single rooms was an undesirable result of the first two concerns. When hospital rooms were out of order, the unsuspecting patients were even occasionally shuffled off to a nearby rival hospital. This was a costly practice that had become commonplace during the busy periods. Glover noticed Bob scribbling on a note pad.

In a very effective summary, the team leader presented the overall costs associated with having Maintenance and Engineering staff spend their time in the car park clearing rubbish. His total cost figure was close to $50,000 per year in revenue lost to the hospital. Most important, he was able to link the misdirected labor costs, out-of-order rooms, and reassigned patients to the rubbish problem.

Bob asked a few questions regarding where the costs were obtained, then congratulated the team on their presentation. "I have to admit that

I did not believe this rubbish problem to be worthy of your time, but apparently I was wrong. No one at the Executive Committee level had any idea of the depth of this problem." He paused for a moment, then continued, "Now what are we going to do about it?"

A Solution

When the team leader suggested the solution to the rubbish problem, Bob and Glover were impressed at its obvious simplicity:

> We realized that the problem was the result of an absence of trash bins in the immediate area of the car park. Our team has made numerous observations of visitors and even hospital staff getting out of their cars to look for a receptacle for fast-food wrappers, unwanted newspapers, and drink containers. When they could not locate a trash bin, they often would toss their rubbish on the pavement. In fact, we even observed several Executive Committee members who discretely dropped rubbish as they walked from their car.

Bob seemed uneasy with the team's last observation, but the proposed solution was compelling:

> What the Maintenance and Engineering team proposes is that four attractive trash bins be purchased and placed at strategic points in the car park. The cost will be $1,600 for the bins. Thus, what we propose is that we can reduce or eliminate the $50,000 in costs associated with the problem by spending $1,600.

Bob responded by thanking the team for their hard work and insightful analysis. "Also, I would like to know if you have other solutions in case the rubbish bins do not solve the problem." The team leaders responded:

> We believe the four bins will resolve the rubbish problem. At this time we do not want to try other options for a solution. In the next 3 months, we will observe and track the problem to see the impact of the rubbish bins being introduced into the car park area. If our solution is not working, we will let you know.

Bob purchased the rubbish bins upon the recommendation of the team. He made a public issue of his support for the team by having a photo of him signing the check for the bins included in the next hospital-employee newsletter.

The solution was tracked for 3 months. Team members grew in confidence each week as the data were reviewed at their meetings. Tracking results indicated that labor costs were being used more appropriately; fewer patient rooms were out of order, and fewer patients were being reassigned to another hospital. Graphics developed by the team indicated a drop in labor costs from $256 per week to $64, as the rubbish bins began to do their jobs. Further, for the previous month, there had been no out-of-order rooms. This led to the reduction in reassigned patients, due to out-of-order rooms, to zero.

The team's cost–benefit analysis was very convincing. Their success and confidence in the process of team problem solving became well known throughout the hospital. Teams in other departments seemed to absorb some of the Maintenance and Engineering team's enthusiasm as they learned of their success. Bob was inspired and could not wait until the next hospital administrators' meeting to tell others of his success.

History Repeats Itself

The hospital was visited by the company president later in the year. Bob proudly invited the president to attend a Maintenance and Engineering team meeting. Prior to the presentation, the president questioned why the rubbish in the car park had been chosen by the team. "Why would they work on an insignificant issue such as rubbish? I understood this team system would make us revenues and improve patient satisfaction." He quizzed Bob and Glover on the way to the meeting. Fortunately, the team had decided to present the entire process involved with the "rubbish in the car park" problem to their high-ranking visitor.

After the presentation, it became apparent that the president had changed his mind on the rubbish issue. He asked a few questions of the team and then congratulated Bob and the team on such an innovative and worthy effort. Bob was definitely on the fast track for promotion.

A Change of Leadership

One year later, Bob was assigned to be the administrator of a new hospital. He left behind a highly motivated and effective group of teams at the hospital. In fact, the union leaders had joined teams and the system appeared to have the full support of all stakeholders. Union problems appeared to be a thing of the past.

Then a new hospital administrator arrived to replace Bob. He had a reputation for being a tough, no-nonsense manager. In his previous assignment, he had cut expenses in the hospital by 20%, primarily via staff reductions. In his initial orientation to the property, he politely listened to the Executive Committee members boast about the teams and positive work environment at the hospital. He was invited to attend a meeting of the Maintenance and Engineering team the following week.

At that meeting, the team leader informed the others that the secretary for the new hospital administrator had just phoned to say that he was too busy to attend. He sent his regards.

As the months passed, it became apparent to the teams that the new administrator did not find much benefit in their efforts. He was heard to make sarcastic remarks at an Executive Committee meeting, "I wish these teams members would concentrate on their real work!" He was simply tolerating the teams, but he did not see much value in what they did. At one meeting he asked the finance manager to provide an analysis of the labor costs associated with the team system.

Within 6 months, the teams were meeting only sporadically. Their department heads were applying subtle pressure to keep their staff in the workplace and out of meetings. These middle managers were fully aware of the hospital administrator's feelings about the teams. Glover made a brief visit to the hospital at the request of the human resources manager. She had been observing the drop in employee morale and team productivity. Glover also spoke with the team leaders, who vented their frustrations with the new administrator.

Afterward, Glover met with the new hospital administrator. He was polite, but kept looking at his watch, as Glover explained the team members' frustrations with his lack of support. Glover showed him the "rubbish in the car park" analysis that the team had prepared a year before, hoping that the financial benefits implied in their work might gain his interest. It did not seem to have an effect on him. It was almost as if he did not believe the financial data before his eyes. After 15 minutes of discussion, he ushered Glover to the door. "Keep in touch," he said. Then he turned quickly to go back to his office. Glover heard a year later that the hospital had some labor unrest and a strike was being considered.

This case illustrates the need to realize change in relationship to employee participation and involvement in problem solving, as well as the need to obtain buy-in from management. It also shows that "the way we do things around here" may have no logical reason behind it, and that new boxes, or ways of doing things, do not have to deal with high-level strategies or boardroom decisions to be important to an organization's success. In addition, this case shows how change initiatives are based on cultural beliefs, stakeholder values, and social dynamics, and those in power within organizations must value change initiatives for them to succeed in the long term. Being able to work successfully with these and similar dynamics is an important part of transcultural competence. Finally, the case illustrates the importance of power and leadership in change initiatives. When Bob left the hospital, the new administrator did not support the teams, and eventually the organizational culture reverted to the old ways of doing things.

7

The Cultures of Those Who Study Culture

To assume that one's own culture is "natural," and to use it as a baseline against which to unfavorably compare other cultures, exemplifies ethnocentrism, the most pervasive cultural blunder. Trying to impose the way things have always been done in one's own culture onto others as the singularly best way for them to do things exacerbates that all-too-common ethnocentric mistake. In this chapter we discuss the importance of understanding and applying cultural principles in various professions seen as cultures.

Understanding that one's own culture is simply one among many cultures—no better or worse in a culturally relative way—is one of the most difficult things in life. This realization is the part of the prerequisite of recognition that is necessary for transcultural competence, as it is important to recognize both one's own cultural baggage as well as others' cultures. Without this crucial insight, cultural differences in others will always be

http://dx.doi.org/10.1037/14596-007
Transcultural Competence: Navigating Cultural Differences in the Global Community, by J. Glover and H. L. Friedman

seen from the biased lens of one's own unquestioned cultural assumptions. Without such recognition, there also can be no real respect, and without respect, there can be no possibility for reconciliation or realization. In these important ways, the 4Rs are interdependent. Understanding one's own culture as being one among many particular cultures provides the basis for knowing that all cultures are simply ways of making sense of, and adapting to, the world. Self-awareness, including how one has been socialized into one's own particular culture with all of its attendant assumptions, is an important beginning step for transcultural competence.

In a classic paper, Horace Miner (1956) convincingly described an exotic tribe, the Nacirema. He explored many of their magical practices, such as those related to a fascination they had with their mouths. The Nacirema voluntarily gave a great deal of wealth to go twice a year, regardless of any perceivable need, to "holy mouth men," who would put them through a ritual of excruciating oral torture. The Nacirema believed that the state of their mouths influenced every sphere of their lives, such as whether they would find a suitable mate, and that unless they religiously attended to this part of their anatomy, their entire lives would be unsuccessful. Consequently, every morning they would pray at a special shrine placed over a fountain of flowing water constructed in a secretive room in their huts by doing elaborate rituals to their mouths involving bristled implements. While doing this mouth ritual, which was a very private practice, they would stare at their own images in a reflective surface mounted over the fountain. Miner similarly described other exotic rituals in this unusual tribe, painting a picture of a bizarre people with unusual beliefs and practices. For those not yet in on the joke, Nacirema is "American" spelled backwards, the holy mouth men are dentists, the bristled implements are toothbrushes, and the shrine is the Western bathroom sink with its accompanying water faucet and mirror.

PROFESSIONS AS CULTURES

Much has been written on becoming aware of national and regional specifics related to culture, such as the appropriateness of what has often been called "kiss, bow, or shake hands" (Morrison & Conoway, 2006) when greeting another based on varying cultural contexts. There has also been much attention given to other cultural specifics, such as ethnicity, religion, and many other relevant statuses. However, there is one particularly important aspect of the cultural baggage of professionals who study and work with culture that has been rarely examined: how the cultures of professional disciplines affect their scholars and practitioners. These disciplinary cultures slant the views and approaches of professionals who are practicing under their auspices, and can be a source of significant bias. Quite frequently, we have seen professionals not only blind to this important aspect of their cultural baggage but who also readily try to impose their limited disciplinary views on others, as if their discipline alone has the unique secrets needed for successfully addressing cultural problems. This is particularly concerning in terms of the cultural biases of people who work as cultural experts from a variety of disciplines that purport to study and understand culture.

Describing Disciplinary Cultures

Professional disciplines, like all organizational forms, have their unique cultures. These have been characterized in many ways, such as distinctions between hard and soft disciplines (Braxton, 1995), between applied and pure disciplines (Squires, 2005), and, most famously, between scientific and humanistic disciplines (Snow, 2012). Based on prior empirical research, Becher and Trowler (2001) portrayed various academic disciplines as "tribes," each with its own history and ways of doing things, something we think quite apt.

We focus on the many disciplines that deal with culture, acknowledging up front that there is considerable variability within these fields. For example, anthropology has many intradisciplinary divisions, for example, between physical anthropologists and prehistorians who study humans in ways more associated with the physical sciences, while social and cultural anthropologists tend to be more aligned with the social sciences. Similarly, sociology has its many intradisciplinary divisions, such as that between demographers who typically work with macroscale population statistics and ethnomethodologists who study microscale interactions using direct observations of behaviors and qualitative narratives on the meaning underlying these behaviors. Psychology also has its many factions, as in its intradisciplinary differences between clinical and research psychologists.

Disciplines also often overlap with related fields; for example, anthropologists, sociologists, and psychologists share many methods related to studying culture. Bernard (2011) noted that all these disciplines use similar methods, at least on occasion, but that, as a broad generalization, traditionally each favors some methods over others: Anthropology favors participant observation, psychology favors experimentation, and sociology favors using survey questionnaires. However, Bernard also noted that the most salient interdisciplinary differences reside in the types of questions being asked, not their methods, concluding that these differences can be meaningfully described as distinct cultures.

In order to encourage recognizing the role of disciplinary cultures for those who study and work with culture, we examine six disciplines strongly involved with culture. Our goal is to help reveal some of their disciplinary characteristics, both as strengths and weaknesses that might affect their professionals' transcultural competence. It is important to note that generalizations about these disciplines do not apply in all cases, and, in terms of cultural relativity applied to these disciplines, no discipline is judged as better or worse overall than others, as all have their respective places.

The fields we selected are the three basic social sciences just mentioned (i.e., anthropology, psychology, and sociology). Of course, these also have many applied practitioners. There are also three more applied disciplines (i.e., management, organizational behavior, and organizational development) that may draw from these basic social sciences. They too have their distinctive cultures. In order to compare these disciplinary cultures, we consider them in terms of the prerequisites fundamental for achieving transcultural competence, as well as their various ways of knowing (both research and applied) across disciplines.

Comparisons Using the Prerequisites

Disciplines can vary in the extent to which they meet the identified prerequisites for transcultural competence, namely, cultural relativity, synchronic and diachronic perspectives, holistic perspectives, and understanding values. For example, Adler (1991) explained how cultural values for individualism and achievement were influential in forming the paradigms for research in which motivation has been studied in the West during the last century. We begin by comparing the six selected disciplines on these prerequisites.

Cultural Relativity

Cultural relativity, as one of the prerequisites for transcultural competence, varies among professional disciplines. Unfortunately, many disciplines whose origins are in Western societies tend to be ethnocentric in their theories and methods for understanding and working with culture and cultural differences. For example, psychology has been often criticized for its ethnocentrism, for example, its frequent overgeneralizing from a narrow range of people studied to all people (Henrich, Heine, & Norenzayan, 2010). The fact that psychology focuses on individuals is contrary to the collectivist approaches of most cultures, and may even imply its very subject matter constitutes a bias, when applied to understanding people in collective cultures. Of course, there are many exceptions, such as the outstanding work of Triandis (1994) and Schein (1992). In contrast, anthropologists and sociologists, to a lesser degree, have had a historical respect for the need to be culturally relative, although early ethnographies from both disciplines evidenced bias at times.

Management has drawn from all of these basic disciplines but has tended to be more influenced by psychology and Western business with their concomitant ethnocentrism. This is also true of organizational behavior. Again, however, there have been numerous exceptions to these generalizations. For examples, the work of Trompenaars and Hampden-Turner (2002) and Hofstede (2005) in management, and Adler (1991) in organizational behavior, provides alternatives to the tendency of professionals in those disciplines to be lacking in cultural relativity. As the last of the six disciplines we examine, organizational development and change (ODC) professionals often attempt to be culturally relative. However, a close examination of the theories and methods in ODC does not always reflect an absence of ethnocentric premises. For example, organizational development professionals often refer to "OD values" (Jones & Brazzel,

2014), many of which they assumed to be universal when indeed they are not. As with all the disciplines examined, there are notable exceptions to ethnocentrism, such as Marshak's (1993) work, which provided culturally relative perspectives.

As part of examining cultural relativity in disciplines, we note that it is also important not to flip from overvaluing one's own culture toward its opposite, namely, embracing another's so-called exotic culture in an uncritical manner. For example, sometimes anthropologists have gone "native" by embracing a new culture they are studying as being better, while abandoning their own. This has occasionally been an occupational hazard in this discipline. Friedman has written on *xenophobia*, related to rejecting religious beliefs from other cultures as inferior and even sinful, which has its shadow in *xenophilia*, which overvalues so-called exotic cultures (e.g., many in the predominantly Judeo-Christian West are converting to Buddhism for its presumed greater purity, whereas many in South Korea who are Buddhists are converting to Christianity for the exact same reason; Friedman, 2009).

Professional Socialization Through Experiences in Other Cultures

The division of labor in all cultures results in some degree of specialization, which starts with socialization. This division may be biologically based, as in childbearing being restricted to females (at least until future technology might erase this constraint), or based on learning specific cultural skills. All professionals also undergo some process of occupational socialization, whether it be informal, as in spending time with a local shaman as an apprentice, or formal, as in being an officially enrolled student attending a university.

Professions in disciplines dealing with culture are similarly socialized in different ways; some of these may be useful and others may simply be conveying misunderstandings about the nature of culture. We think learning about culture in the abstract, as in reading ethnographies or other works, can be useful, but this is no substitute for direct experience in different cultures.

The disciplines we examine that train cultural experts, especially in the United States, seldom provide cross- or multicultural immersion experiences. Although it is not uncommon to be superficially exposed to cultures different from their own, students in these disciplines often lack the deep exposure needed to really engage with other cultures. More immersive cultural experiences may challenge professionals to adapt in unexpected ways that a formal curriculum could never provide, influencing a professional's cultural knowledge and skills. First, having to experience and learn a culture different from one's own leads to self-reflection and a better understanding of one's own culture. Second, immersion in a culture different from one's own enables professionals to develop more effective perspectives for working with the challenges of heterogeneous societies and culturally diverse situations. For example, in an immersion experience, professionals will need to question previously held assumptions, and adapt behaviors to be successful in different sociocultural contexts.

Cultural and social anthropologists have long considered working in a culture different from their own to be a necessary requirement for rec-ognition as a professionally trained anthropologist. One strength of their preparation as professionals is that they were expected to immerse them-selves in a culture other than their own as part of graduate studies, often for several years. This ethnographic fieldwork requirement was tradition-ally assumed to enable those in training to better understand their own culture from direct experiences in a different one. As doctoral students, they often would go to great lengths to adapt, or even just to survive, in culturally new settings, as they usually did not initially understand the basics, such as language and expectations for behavior. Unfortunately, although it is still often required, this immersion requirement has not been as universally applied in the education of cultural and social anthro-pologists in recent decades.

Immersion in other cultures has not been part of the professional requirements for many other professional disciplines, even those that purport to foster cultural expertise. Sociology may have that expecta-tion occasionally, but it is not universally expected, whereas psychology, management, organizational behavior, and organization development are disciplines in which immersion in another culture is simply not custom-arily expected as a necessary part of professional education and training.

Corporate expatriate training and university study abroad are attempts to provide some ideas of what to expect in new cultural situations. However, many of these programs do not provide the immersion needed. The expatriate executive or study-abroad student learns by trial and error once thrown into the new environment, but often these experiences are buffered by insulation within cultural enclaves, such as an English-speaking dormitory for students visiting a non–English-speaking culture.

The lack of such direct cultural immersion for professionals trained in most disciplines that purport to know about culture is at the heart of many instances of confusion, faulty perspectives, and biased methodologies for understanding and applying culture in the real world. It is difficult to comprehend the complexities and dynamics of culture when professionals have only seen it from their own cultural vantage. Globalization and technology have created an ever-increasing and challenging heterogeneous environment for professionals from all disciplines. The new global environment has created challenges for all people faced with working with others who do not share their beliefs, values, and expectations. Professionals from disciplines that ignore these types of experiences may be limited in their development of transcultural competence and should consider seeking out such experiences before claiming to be cultural experts.

Achieving Synchronic and Diachronic Perspectives

As previously discussed, synchronic perspectives look at people in the present broadly across space (e.g., cross-culturally), whereas diachronic perspectives look at people throughout time (e.g., through tradition and history). Transcultural competence requires both of these time and space perspectives. As an example, also previously mentioned, to understand how humans make decisions requires looking across different cultures (using a synchronic perspective), which includes all the relevant methods and processes for decision making used by humans, not just ones taken from a narrow context such as one culture. When decision making is observed across the continuum of human culture that exists in the contemporary global community, a wide range of cultural perspectives and practices for making decisions are found. Someone from the United States who wants to negotiate a contract in other cultures may become very frustrated because U.S. contractual models for negotiations and decision making are not practiced universally. Any professional and/or discipline following or advocating for only one model for decision making for all humans lacks transcultural competence.

A classic synchronic approach to understanding culture is the "Human Relations Area Files" originally developed by George Murdock (1967). Hundreds of ethnographic reports on human societies from around the world have been classified in this database, from the 1930s to the present (see http://www.yale.edu/hraf/). Comparing how humans in different cultures make decisions, are motivated, and attend meetings are just a few of many different situations in which comparisons across cultures can prevent ethnocentrically flawed explanations for culture and its expressions.

Diachronic perspectives are based on an understanding of cultural evolution and how it has transformed the human experience. Prehistory (e.g., archeology), history, and other related disciplines provide abundant information on the human journey through time. One particular human dynamic through time is the movement from homogeneous (e.g., bands, tribal societies) to heterogeneous (e.g., nation-states, urban, and complex societies) sociocultural contexts. By understanding this and other essential transformations, such as the development of food production and urban settlements from food extraction and nomadic patterns, perplexing cultural dilemmas can often be understood. Much of the world's current turmoil can be grasped by understanding Colonial and post-Colonial experiences, as many current nations were arbitrarily formed from components that do not fit together well, as they include many formerly independent political units, cultural groups, and languages. The world news gives daily reminders of this Colonial and post-Colonial forced mix of ethnic, religious, and cultural groups by colonial administrators who gave little consideration to cultural differences among the people who already occupied these countries. Thus, an understanding of the human experience through time and space has much to offer in dealing with current cultural differences and avoiding the errors of the past.

Managers and practitioners of organizational behavior and organizational development, as well as psychologists, typically have limited perspectives on the human experience through time and space. Regarding time, anthropologists, and to a lesser degree sociologists, often take a more long-term approach to understanding people, such as exploring not just what is, but also how it came to be. In contrast, studying people in a historical perspective and comparing them with people in other cultures is rare for psychologists (e.g., Henrich, Heine, & Norenzayan, 2010). The disciplines of management, organizational behavior, and organizational development also do not give much value to diachronic perspectives, although there is often value given to synchronic research and applications (e.g., Adler & Gundersen, 2008; Hofstede, 2005; Trompenaars, 2012). Using both time and space perspectives is a prerequisite for the transcultural competence of professionals and within these various disciplines. Without such perspectives, understandings are similar to photos taken in one location at one point in time: The scene in the photo may be interesting to the viewer, but the world around it is not shown.

Achieving Holistic Perspectives

Understanding holism is also an important prerequisite for transcultural competence. In professional practice, a failure to see the "bigger picture" in a cultural context may lead to unanticipated consequences.

Anthropology is usually seen as holistic in that it deals with many important dimensions of people (e.g., evolutionary, biological–physical, cultural, economic, social, psychological). Sociology also considers a wide range of cultural influences on human behavior and experience, but it rarely includes the relationship of biology to culture. In contrast, psychology tends to deal primarily with experiences and behaviors in individuals in an isolated decontextualized way and tends to lack a holistic perspective. Management, organizational behavior, and organizational development advocate the understanding of systems and apply those systems dynamics to understanding organizations. Unfortunately, some systems approaches may not include a big-picture approach where culture is a consideration. It is not uncommon to hear professionals from those fields describe an organizational model based on structure, strategy, processes, and culture, but fail to realize that organizations are cultures, and that culture is not something an organization "has," but something an organization "is" (Sackmann, 1991).

Applying Values

Cross-cultural studies have revealed many important cultural-values dimensions, and being able to use these is important for transcultural competence. Although there are many value dimensions that can be explored, we refocus here on only the universal–particular and individual–collective dimensions to illustrate how the values of disciplinary professionals influence their transcultural competence.

Universal–Particular *Universalism* involves wanting everything to be uniform, without exceptions. For example, a discipline's focus on finding "laws" that account for all cultural differences would be a universal attempt. *Particularism* involves respecting variations by not attempting to find invariances across all settings. An example of particularism is a recent intervention in Zimbabwe, in which Friedman consulted (Machinga & Friedman, 2013). In designing a program to help former child soldiers reconcile back into their communities, Friedman recognized that there are two distinct cultures relevant to such an intervention in Zimbabwe, namely, people with indigenous (Shona) and Western (Christian) values. Rather than providing one intervention, two distinct reconciliations programs, each fitted to the appropriate cultural values, were provided.

Universalism may influence people who do not share that value orientation to behave in unusual ways. When working with local governmental officials in a South American country, a colleague noted that one official did not seem to understand him when he spoke Dutch. The official was always smiling and nodding his head as the colleague spoke to him. The colleague left the official's office thinking that meetings had gone well, despite the fact that he had done most of the talking. However, none of our colleague's requests were ever put into effect by the official.

On one visit to the official, our colleague tried to communicate in the local language. When the official became visibly upset that the colleague had spoken to him in his native language, our colleague asked an associate what he thought the problem was. The colleague learned that in that country, speaking Dutch was a sign of an educated and urbane person. Those who spoke the local language were considered to be "lower class" peasant farmers. His friend explained that even though the official did not understand Dutch, he did not want anyone to know. When the colleague spoke to him in the local language, he had insulted the official. From a universal perspective, it would be reasonable to assume that speaking to someone in a language they did not know well would be inappropriate, but in this particular context it was appropriate.

Values for universalism are often observed as management, psychology, organizational behavior, and organizational development professionals attempt to apply the idea that "one size fits all." Team designs, group dynamics, pay-for-performance systems, and motivation and incentive programs are generally based on Western values of individualism and achievement. The designers of those programs usually assume that everyone is universally motivated by the same values. Anthropologists and sociologists, in contrast, commonly recognize the importance of differing values orientations.

Individual–Collective Values for individualism may bias professionals if they fail to realize the influence of collectivism on many humans. Adler and Gundersen (2008) pointed out that most motivation theories in use today were developed in the United States by and about Americans. Of those that were not, many have been influenced by U.S. theoretical work. These theories do not offer universal explanations of motivation; rather, they reflect the individualistic value system of Americans. They summarized this, as follows:

> Unfortunately, American as well as non-American managers have tended to treat American theories as the best or only way to understand motivation. They are neither. American motivation theories, although assumed to be universal in their reliance on individualism as a motivator, have failed to provide consistently useful explanations outside the United States. Professionals must therefore guard against imposing domestic American management theories on their multinational business practices. (pp. 161–162)

Unfortunately, the management, organizational behavior, and psychology disciplines have historically used theories and methods influenced by their own values, such as for individualism, without often recognizing this bias. In contrast, sociology and anthropology have generally recognized how values may influence their study of culture, as even ethnographic studies that strive to be value-free have been shown to be influenced by their researchers' worldviews.

Advocacy

Advocacy is a specific example, related to values, as it means asserting a value position. Everyone can understand having an agenda, such as in business to maximize profit or market share and in the military to expand a range of interest or protection, but many professionals in the area of culture assume it is desirable to impose their own values in another cultural setting if these are congruent with their image of doing "good." Of course, this is the same reasoning used by missionaries to convert others by the sword, including killing them in the name of providing them a better "afterlife."

Understanding a profession's relationship to advocacy in assuming various values positions is important for achieving transcultural competence. From a perspective of cultural relativity, there is simply no reason to privilege any set of values over another, just as it makes little sense to be angry at a wolf for eating a sheep: From the wolf's position, this is a good thing, while from the sheep's, this is a bad thing. Taking value positions can lead to passionate advocacy on one side of an issue while ignoring its opposite.

Illustrations of professionals demonstrating advocacy positions are common. Glover attended an anthropology conference in which solutions for health problems in rural migrant farmworkers were being discussed. The anthropologists making the presentation discussed data they thought relevant to the problems, but these data had been gathered only from the farmworkers. The lack of data relevant to farm owners and other community members was obvious. Glover suggested that similar data from the farm owners and other stakeholders in the community would be useful in developing a more holistic perspective on the problems being discussed. This invoked the ire of many on the panel of anthropologists, who clearly saw the farmworkers' plight but, as advocates for only one side of a complex whole, did not see any legitimacy in involving the community stakeholders and farm owners' perspectives in the solution.

We think all the disciplines considered commonly promote advocacy as part of their professional cultures. These are often promoted as ethical codes, which grant them a perceived legitimacy that simply may not be in accord with their applications in various cultural contexts. We include advocacy as an important part of understanding values for transcultural competency because embracing one side of a dilemma to the exclusion of another, especially if justified by an ideological position, is a common problem.

A Comparison of Worldviews of Professions That Study Culture

In Table 7.1, we provide a way to summarize our discussion of selected disciplines relevant to transcultural competence, as well as provide a tentative categorization for heuristic purposes of their disciplinary biases. We also emphasize that we consider the importance of awareness of one's disciplinary culture to be equal to, or perhaps more important than, awareness of other aspects of one's culture for a professional working in the area of culture. Although the classification provided is based only on our professional impressions, it is our tentative way to begin to make sense of this complex concern. There are many ways that the fundamental assumptions, or worldviews, used in various disciplinary approaches to culture can be understood, so Table 7.1 is not exhaustive of all possible ways, nor is it what we would necessarily suggest as the best way to organize this information. However, we believe that presenting the aspects of each discipline's worldview in the table highlights many of the most important prerequisites for transcultural competence in a useful comparative way and also addresses the case we present at this chapter's end.

Professionals from all disciplines who wish to practice, conduct research, and teach others about culture should understand the importance of each prerequisite for transcultural competence. Our hope is that our initial approach for analyzing the worldviews of these professional disciplines that study and work with culture will also provide a useful starting point for stimulating further research and discussion.

Table 7.1

Fundamental Perspectives of Select Disciplines That Study Culture

Fundamental perspective (worldview)	Psychology	Anthropology	Management	Sociology	Organizational behavior	Organizational development
Holism	Uncommon	Common	Uncommon	Common	Uncommon	Uncommon
Diachronic	Uncommon	Common	Uncommon	Occasionally	Uncommon	Uncommon
Synchronic	Uncommon	Common	Uncommon	Occasionally	Occasionally	Occasionally
Cultural Relativity	Uncommon	Common	Uncommon	Common	Uncommon	Uncommon
Values of Researchers (using only two value dimensions)	Universalism/ Individualism	Particularism/ Collectivism	Universalism/ Individualism	Particularism/ Collectivism	Universalism/ individualism	Universalism/ Collectivism
Ways of Knowing (research methods)	Psychometric	Cultural Metric	Psychometric	Sociometric	Psychometric	Psychometric

CASE ANALYSIS: UNDERSTANDING
DIFFERENT WAYS OF KNOWING

We were in a meeting with a group of consultants working on a U.S. Department of Defense project, and the discussion focused on designing a program to train cross-cultural competence in soldiers. When the question of assessing training outcomes came up, in order to know if the training being designed would be useful, members of the group proposed a variety of self-report questionnaires commonly used to measure cross-cultural competence. These questionnaires typically asked respondents to numerically rate how much they agreed with various items, such as, "I feel uncomfortable with people from cultures different than my own," which were then combined mathematically into scales yielding numbers supposedly operationalizing differing dimensions of cross-cultural competence. We asked whether people who were more willing to endorse feeling uncomfortable around those from other cultures might be the ones who were actually more culturally competent. We pointed out that perhaps the ones who would be uncomfortable were the ones who adaptively recognized how easy it can be for misunderstandings and other problems to arise during cross-cultural sociocultural encounters (SCEs), while those feeling comfortable might be the ones who were most oblivious to the many pitfalls in such encounters. Our concern was met with puzzled looks, as using self-reports as the standard for measurement was commonplace by the professional consultants within that setting.

Instead, we proposed using interactive measures based on actual SCEs of warfighters with "local" peoples, such as Afghan village elders (Friedman et al., 2013). This approach would involve putting trainees into simulations and observing how they responded when presented with complex cultural dilemmas to which there are no simple answers. When proposing this dilemmas-based assessment by offering some alternatives to self-report assessment, there was limited understanding of this "alien" approach. For example, when we proposed relevant dilemmas to use in simulations to assess cultural competence, some of the so-called cultural experts in the group kept asking, "But what are the right answers to the dilemmas?" Of course, by definition dilemmas do not have right answers, or they would not be dilemmas.

Disciplines vary in their approaches to what is considered an appropriate way for knowing something like the effectiveness of a training program. Of course, these preferences vary not just by disciplines but also by cultural factors, such as prevailing national and organizational paradigms, as reflected in the unique culture of the consultants for the U.S. Department of Defense.

One way to illustrate this is to look at how three disciplines, namely, psychology, anthropology, and sociology, use assessment in relationship to culture. We call each a type a *metric*, even though assessment is not always quantitative. *Psychometrics* is based on assumptions that the individual should be seen as the primary unit of analysis in understanding culture and that precise quantitative measurement is more valuable than nuanced qualitative description. *Sociometrics*, in contrast, looks at the interactions of individuals, such as relationships within a social network, not the individuals themselves, and these can be portrayed mathematically, descriptively, and using both methods. *Cultural metrics* is a term we use to describe more holistic approaches to culture, and also can be portrayed numerically, narratively, or using mixed methods. Cultural metrics uses assessment approaches designed to study culture, not self-reported attitudes and beliefs of individuals "about" how they see culture.

Using self-report questionnaires to assess an individual's cultural competence as a set of knowledge, skills, and abilities is psychometric, and favored by many psychologists and practitioners of organizational behavior. However, there are many problems in using psychometric methods, especially across cultures. For example, many cultures consider it rude to express disagreement, so asking participants from such cultures to rate items in terms of scales of *agree* to *disagree* could be culturally inappropriate by forcing people to act in ways they consider rude, which of course would make the validity of their responses questionable. However, when effectively developed, there are also many advantages to psychometric approaches; for example, they can be used to quickly harvest and analyze large amounts of data in a way that appears scientific.

Looking at interactive variables would be more sociometric. As an example, when consulting in Fiji, we looked to measure the ways in which hotels offered hospitality, and we decided to focus on how their employees interacted with us as customers, not knowing we were consultants. To operationalize this, rather than using a complex psychometric survey coming up with precise numbers of dubious worth, we decided to use a simple strategy. The term *bula* in Fiji means hello, goodbye, and a number of other things, and we used it to serve as a rough way to assess the overall level of hospitality within Fijian hotels. Consequently, as we visited hotels with which we were working, we simply counted the number of bulas that were given to us as we walked around the properties. We also recorded the number of instances in which we did not receive a bula, especially when it would have been expected. We found it to relate to other "harder" indicators (e.g., profits, labor–management relations) of how well these properties were faring. Although an alternative approach to measurement, we found it quite useful. Anthropologists and sociologists, as well as some organizational development professions, may be observed to use this type of ethnographic approach, but psychologists would probably dismiss this as lacking scientific rigor.

As an example of cultural metrics, during the 1990s we were involved in a global research project to understand organizational culture. As part of this effort, we provided comprehensive organizational assessments within more than 30 corporations, governments, and communities across over a dozen nations by measuring various aspects of organizational cultures. All departments and levels of the organizations were assessed, using qualitative focus groups, participant observations, and individually structured interviews, along with quantitative survey results and archival data indicating various ways the organizations were performing. The results of each organizational assessment were a profile of cultural metrics developed and discussed with the leaders and other stakeholders in the organization. Unfortunately, such comprehensive methods are seldom used. One problem with such an approach, however, is that it can be very costly in terms of time and resources. However, good, rather than convenient, data are often worth the cost.

It is important to recognize that methods for obtaining information about the world are generally part of the disciplinary culture in which those methods are used. In addition, what is interpreted from such information also tends to be framed within the cultural perspectives of a discipline. Therefore, what professionals claim to know, as well as how they go about knowing and applying knowledge, is a reflection of their professional disciplinary culture.

8

Applications of Transcultural Competence

Transcultural competence is needed in a wide variety of organizations and other contexts. Cultural beliefs and values are both reflected in and shape the design and delivery of goods and services through social institutions, and consequently they vary widely across differing cultural contexts. Social institutions deal with how people cooperate to meet the demands of existence and survival. We use economic and community development, education, mental health, and health care to illustrate how essential it is for professionals who work within these social institutions to be transculturally competent.

As previously pointed out, all people need to eat, but how they eat, what they eat, with whom and when they eat, and many other nuances of eating are culturally relative. Eating involves how humans deal with subsistence and other material necessities. Economic and community development provides our first example of an application of transcultural competence.

http://dx.doi.org/10.1037/14596-008
Transcultural Competence: Navigating Cultural Differences in the Global Community, by J. Glover and H. L. Friedman

ECONOMIC AND COMMUNITY DEVELOPMENT

Cultural evolution has led to the development of and successive changes in all social institutions. Professionals working in community and economic development initiatives frequently encounter stakeholders with cultural differences that affect their agendas. For example, in Chapter 3 we discussed stakeholders' differing orientations to fundamental economic exchange principles of reciprocity, redistribution, and the market principal (Polanyi, 1944). Cultural values orientations related to these exchange principles are often the source of dilemmas that may emerge as development programs are planned and implemented. Such dilemmas are apparent in the Blue Horizon case, the expatriate and the village chief case, and others discussed in earlier chapters.

CASES OF CULTURALLY INFLUENCED MODELS FOR ECONOMICS AND BUSINESS

Transcultural competence involves recognizing and respecting different economic systems, as well as being able to reconcile them and realize adaptive ways to apply them. The comparison of some emerging and evolving national economic systems in Table 8.1 illustrates how various contemporary governments have attempted to reconcile the dilemma of socialist and capitalist thought, showing that none of these broad principles are in fact pure types, since they differ in their many cultural expressions. Note that all systems included in the table are currently competing within the global economy. However, the economic models they use vary, for example, on the cultural-values dimensions of individualism and collectivism.

In much of the contemporary West and Westernized cultures, economic activity is channeled through the social institution of business, but businesses come in many different types, such as for-profit versus nonprofit, service versus manufacturing, nations versus other nations (e.g., Japanese vs. United States), national versus international, and so forth. How business is conducted varies considerably, and it takes considerable transcultural competence to negotiate business arrangements across cultural divides.

Table 8.1

Contemporary Economic Models of Capitalism

Model for the practice of capitalism	Ownership system	Corporate community responsibility	Macroeconomic influence on leadership decisions	Time orientation
Individual (British, U.S.)	Shareholders with no loyalty; continual trading	Limited responsibility to society; resistance to government controls	Shareholder value is primary; other stakeholders not considered	Short-term, overnight turn-over of share ownership; immediate
Codetermination (Germany)	Shared among banks, government, and corporations	Corporate and government responsibility is legally mandated	Shareholders and stake-holders cooperate; labor sits on board of directors	Longer term than the United States
Keiretsu (Japan)	Groups of interlocking companies; majority of shares not traded	Loyalty to workers and workers "belong" to company	Harmony and balance critical; autocratic consensus ("ringi" system)	Long-term; investment in research and development even in down times
Chaebol (South Korea)	Government-supported conglomerates; cross-ownership	Corporation is an extension of the government	Government reviews plans of corporations; closely directed	Long-term; government and banks invest in corporate research and development

(continued)

Table 8.1

Contemporary Economic Models of Capitalism (*Continued*)

Model for the practice of capitalism	Ownership system	Corporate community responsibility	Macroeconomic influence on leadership decisions	Time orientation
Government Directed (Singapore)	Government-regulated development; planned economy and investment of government in education of workers	Corporate social responsibility high	Corporations involve government as stakeholder	Long-term; government planning is central focus
Modified Communist (Peoples Republic of China)	Government-controlled joint ventures with outside investors or companies, combination of state and individual enterprises	State is primary benefactor in redistributive economy	Government and joint venture partners decide	Long-term; government directs the course of the future
Fiji	Conflicting models of individual and collective capitalism	Conflicting models of individual and collective capitalism	Traditional Fijian and British–U.S. model in conflict	Village is synchronic, outsiders are sequential

Note. From "The Burdens of Other People's Models: A Cultural Perspective on the Current Fiji Crisis," by H. Friedman, G. Glover, and F. Avegalio, 2002, *Harvard Asia Pacific Review*, 6, p. 89. Copyright 2002 by Harvard Asia Pacific Review. Reprinted with permission.

What on the surface can seem very familiar to someone from one culture might be perceived as having quite different significance in another culture (Hampden-Turner & Trompenaars, 1993).

EDUCATIONAL MODELS AND INSTITUTIONS

As a social institution, education is also built on cultural assumptions that vary within and across cultures. Education can be conducted in a formal manner, such as starting and ending at a given time within a designated setting like a school, or it can be a more informal process, such as an apprenticeship in which the learner actively observes and participates as a helper with someone more experienced. In a formal setting, education would be seen as more specific in its value orientation, while informally it would be more diffuse, such as in how a student might show deference to a schoolteacher specifically while in school, whereas an apprentice might have a more diffusely deferential relationship that extends in various settings with the one providing the mentoring. In many traditions, for example, apprentices live with their mentors and serve as their personal attendants in a variety of tasks, such as running errands and cleaning their residences. In early human societies, education was based on socialization via role models, peer influence, and family-based experiential learning. In contemporary societies, education is usually formalized and structured in classroom and other activities, although learning still occurs in informal traditional methods.

Learning as Individuals or in Groups?

Many divergent values can be observed in education within the global community. In individualistic cultures, students would usually be expected to learn alone, whereas in collectivistic cultures, shared learning in teams would be more likely. Similarly, evaluation of learning would tend to be focused on tests taken and individually written papers, within more individualistic cultures, while it would tend to be more based on group evaluations within more collectivistic cultures. As one extreme difference, working collectively might be seen as "cooperating" in some cultural settings and rewarded, but seen as "cheating" in others in which individuals are expected to do their own work, neither helping nor receiving help from others. While teaching culturally diverse graduate-level classes in a U.S. university, we both noted that East Asian students commonly seemed to have little concern about taking material from the Internet for use in their schoolwork without citing their sources. This reflected a cultural difference, as the sense of intellectual property belonging to an individual (and requiring citation to acknowledge that ownership) was foreign to students from certain collectivist cultures in which ideas were more freely shared than in the culture of a U.S. university, where this behavior is seen as plagiarism.

There are many other educational differences across cultures, such as how some cultures encourage learning in which questions are actively asked and teachers' views are sometimes even challenged. In other cultures, however, students are expected to be passive recipients of knowledge from a teacher. In those cultures, asking a question would be seen as a rude challenge to a teacher. In working with East Asian graduate students, we both found that the U.S. model of graduate symposia in which students are encouraged to actively engage in discussions with their teachers simply did not work well at first, as these students were very hesitant to interact in violation of their cultural norms. Gaining active participation from students accustomed to passively participating in a classroom required the teacher to find ways to reconcile the two styles of learning so all students felt comfortable with open dialogue and even questioning the teacher.

HEALTH CARE: DIFFERENT CULTURAL MODELS OF DISEASE

In settings such as the United States, Western medicine is prevalent and the basis for treatment of physical illness in the general population. However, the majority of the world's population is treated for physical illness using non-Western (indigenous) approaches. In many cases, these approaches are quite successful. Practices using traditional herbs and physical interventions (e.g., acupuncture) may be understood in very different frameworks than provided by Western science. These frameworks have often evolved over millennia of cultural experimentation delineating what works well from what does not work. The rationale for effectiveness of these healing interventions may be articulated in ways that do not make sense to most modern Westerner medical practitioners, but this does not mean that the use of traditional non-Western medical systems is arbitrary or unhelpful. In fact, much of Western medicine has been derived from these traditional uses. For example, aspirin was developed after observing the medicinal effects of willow bark. Certain traditional healing practices employ the bark of the tree from which aspirin is produced in treating a variety of maladies, a practice developed by the ancient Greeks.

In some traditional healing practices, an herb may be understood as possessing a helpful plant spirit that can guide the human toward retrieval of a lost spirit (and any biochemical mechanisms, if recognized, may not be seen as relevant). Acupuncture may be seen as a way to balance subtle energies not amenable to empirical observation (and any effect on modulating the nervous or other biological systems, even if recognized, may not be seen as relevant). These usages have culturally evolved through long periods of trial and error, as well as through concerted searches for cures to ailments. Despite the fact that many of these interventions are very effective, in the contemporary West they tend to be dismissed as only "complementary and alternative" to approaches seen as mainstream, even when they appear to successfully treat a variety of maladies, including some conditions that Western medicine cannot treat.

Germ Theory

A prototypical Western approach to medicine involves the germ theory, namely, the belief that illnesses are often caused by things that are too small to see with the naked eye. *Germs* refer to a variety of small pathogens, including bacteria, viruses, and other microscopic life. After the invention of the microscope, many types of germs became visible, and subsequently they became widely accepted as a major cause of disease. However, even the well-established germ theory has its limits, such as in the case of "strep" throat. A contemporary Western physician can take a sample culture of someone's throat and observe through the technology provided by a microscope a proliferation of *Streptococci* bacteria, which can lead to a diagnosis of "strep" throat and a resulting intervention to kill these germs with an antibiotic. However, many healthy people also have *Streptococci* as part of their ordinary throat flora and these may not only be benign, but even necessary for health. When these germs have proliferated beyond their ordinary level, which could be due to many fundamental reasons (e.g., a lowered state of immune system activation due to stress, since a normal immunity level would ordinarily keep these germs in balance), it may be correlated with illness. Correlation, of course, does not mean causation, and poisoning the bloom of *Streptococci* with antibiotics might solve the immediate problem but not address its root. It also might create new problems, which may be dismissed as only being "side effects," such as gastrointestinal issues related to collaterally killing beneficial organisms in the flora.

Alternatives to Germ Theory

The simple application of the germ theory as the cause of disease clearly has its limits. A more sophisticated Western approach to disease causation is based on epidemiologic theory. Although this acknowledges that germs are agents of disease with important causative features (e.g., infectivity, pathogenicity, virulence), the environment is viewed as also playing a key role in the harm from any germ. From an epidemiological perspective, diseases are seen from a more holistic perspective as having multiple causes.

Throughout the world, many people do not accept germ theory and other so-called scientific explanations of disease. Instead, there are many healing traditions based on widely varying premises that lead to very different practices. Health care may be delivered by specialists, such as Western physicians, or by generalists, such as a grandmother who performs many duties in a village and is also the designated village midwife. Health care can be seen as part of the natural order or as vested in supernatural healing forces. It can be delivered in specialized settings, such as medical offices and hospitals, or wherever it might be needed. Providers of health care can be held in high esteem and greatly rewarded or can be seen as in relatively low-status occupations, as they often have to deal with unpleasant circumstances involving bodily fluids that can elicit disgust. They can also be feared, as the power to heal can also be equated with the power to harm. Transcultural competence involving health care as a social institution calls upon recognizing and respecting these cultural differences, as well as reconciling them to realize adaptive outcomes.

In India, many people rely on traditional *Ayurvedic* theories of healing, and the popularity of this approach is increasing in the West (Mukherjee, 2001). It is based on seeking a balance in a subtle energy (*prana*) that takes three primary forms related to health: movement (*vata* or wind), transformation (*pitta* or fire), and structure (*kapha* or earth). These are seen as affecting body, environment, mind, and spirit, and while the goal of Ayurveda is not so much to heal disease, although that can be its focus, it is to teach people to live a balanced life according to its theory. There are a variety of ways to balance these energies through Ayurvedic techniques, such as by eating foods that can increase or decrease these energies in helpful ways, or by using aromatherapy, massage, meditation, and yogic postures that are thought to sedate some, and stimulate other, energies.

Another widely followed approach to healing is Traditional Chinese Medicine, and it has many variants throughout cultures in Eastern Asia, where it is widely practiced alongside Western medicine (Hesketh & Zhu, 1997). It is also becoming increasingly popular in the West. It is based on the notion of a life energy (*chi*) that can be more or less *yin* (feminine) and *yang* (masculine) and that also requires balance for health. Stimulation of certain points on the skin by needles (acupuncture) or massage (acupressure), or through the application of heat or other methods, can be used in this healing system to balance chi. In addition, exercises such as *Tai Chi* (a slow-moving meditation), sitting meditation, and other practices can also be used in Traditional Chinese Medicine. One interesting difference between this approach and contemporary Western medicine involves the way in which services are traditionally paid for. In the West, people are expected to pay for treatment when they are ill, whereas in Traditional

Chinese Medicine people are expected to pay when they are well: When they become sick, the practitioner is expected to pay the patient for the failure of the preventive approach.

Although there is growing evidence that the both Ayurveda and Traditional Chinese Medicine can be helpful, our point is not to compare them for efficacy. Rather, it is to show that there are important cultural differences in how health care is conceptualized and provided, and these must be recognized, respected, and reconciled to realize adaptive ways to work with health and disease. Even in the contemporary West, many individuals and groups rely on notions such as spiritual causation and imbalances in subtle energy, as well as many other explanatory frameworks that veer from mainstream Western biomedicine. Privileging Western conceptions of health and illness as the only way to understand and treat disease, while dismissing other approaches because their rationale might not be congruent with Western understandings is ethnocentric. This is not meant to deny the value of much of Western medicine, but seeks instead to broaden its perceived worth in relationship to a larger transculturally competent framework that recognizes and respects other cultural approaches as also having value. When there are dilemmas related to differing worldviews and belief systems related to health care, these require reconciliation to realize effective outcomes.

Patient Compliance in a Migrant Health Clinic

Glover served on the board of directors for a migrant health clinic. He observed an ongoing issue in the effectiveness of treatments prescribed for its patients. The two medical doctors working there were trained in Western medicine and were quite different from the migrants in their sociocultural backgrounds. The migrants came from the Caribbean and Mexico, and did not understand the beliefs and practices of Western medicine. The migrants went to the clinic when they were ill because they were ordered by their patrons and farm owners to do so. The medical doctors were unable to communicate effectively in the native language of the migrants. The result of these cultural differences between the medical staff and the migrants was low patient compliance with recommended treatments. For example, patients would often not have prescriptions filled and, even when they did fill them, would not take the medications as directed. The migrants did not understand or believe in the germ theory of disease. The medical doctors did not understand the cultural beliefs of the migrants regarding disease. They dismissed "obeah" and "voodun" and other supernaturally based beliefs held by the patients as mere superstitions and gave them no credibility.

Although it never happened at the time, the clinic could have benefitted greatly by developing and training cultural brokers who could bridge the gap between the Western-trained medical doctors and the migrant patients. The brokers would be able to "translate" between the two models of disease causation. This bridging approach was initially developed in Navajo medical clinics in the 1970s (Adair, Deuschle, & Barnett, 1988), and it provided an effective reconciliation of the Navaho and Western models of health care. In this model, traditional healers and Western practitioners worked together in providing healing. Unfortunately, however, it was unsuccessful in changing health care delivery to the Navajo in a sustainable way, as the U.S. Public Health Service soon abandoned this innovative strategy, despite its success. The failure to realize these results on a long-term basis was attributed by the developers to their being unable to adequately advocate for its implementation within the larger government bureaucracy, which was vested in only Western ways of understanding and delivering health care.

MENTAL HEALTH

Although the concept of mental illness is embedded within a system of beliefs and values deemed "scientific" by Western cultures (and therefore presumably universally applicable across time and space to all humans), in fact, it is a culturally relative attribute. Mental illness is based on layers of complex metaphysical assumptions that vest certain types of problems as being "illnesses." These understandings are no better or worse on any absolute grounds than are many culturally competing theories, such as "spirit loss" being the cause of such problems (Sam & Moreira, 2002).

Mental illness is a cultural construct without any "objective" way to diagnose or treat it. It rests within the history of Western dualism, namely, the belief that there exists a "mental" that somehow is apart from the physical. Stemming back to antiquity in Western culture, this separation of mind and body underlies the Western belief in the reality of mental illness. Of course, the notion of spirit loss is also based on a dualism between body and spirit.

Although biomedical approaches, such as favored in most of contemporary Western psychiatry, attempt to reduce the mental to just an epiphenomenon of brain, the underlying networks of cultural assumptions and meanings related to something presumably disembodied pervade the area. In addition, what is seen as mental illness from a Western perspective and spirit loss from a Southeast Asian context (Sam & Moreira, 2002) may not be seen as a problem at all within other cultural contexts. For example, an individual with what would be likely seen as mental illness in the West could in some parts of rural India be seen as "god-intoxicated" and revered as a highly evolved spiritual being, rather than seen as a pitiful one afflicted with a debilitating problem. The treatment received by someone with this type of presentation in rural India might involve devoted care aimed at encouraging continuing communion with god as a positive event, rather than aimed at eliminating it as a problem. Such care could include lovingly bestowing the god-intoxicated one with garlands of flowers, while worshipping that one as a sacred manifestation of divinity.

As one of the many specialized areas of health care, mental health is based on models that differ widely across cultures. It provides an especially good case for examining cultural differences, as most contemporary Western cultures view the causes of mental illness as stemming from what is deemed a privileged scientific perspective that allegedly captures the "truth" of the matter. However, there is little evidence to award such status to Western models of mental illness, and all approaches to mental health and illness can be seen as culturally relative, including those based on so-called scientific understandings. They also all may be adaptive in their cultural context to the relative degree that they work in meeting human needs. In the West, causes of mental illness usually revolve around some combination of biological, psychological, and social explanations, whereas in other cultures, causation is often attributed to transgressions from past lives, imbalances in subtle energies, and spirit loss or possession by an evil spirit, as well as by some other lack of harmony with the world.

Transcultural competence in mental health professionals and organizations requires being able to understand and adaptively operate within and across various social institutions. Mental health care, as one social institution, benefits from a culturally relative and synchronic view across different cultures, as the examples illustrate. To understand mental health care as a social institution also requires a diachronic view across time, such as provided by discussing the historical relationship of the term mental to the term *spirit.*

Mental health care is also closely interrelated to other social institutions and needs to be approached holistically. It is part of larger systems of care, such as health care in general, as well as the even larger overarching social institution called human services. It is also inextricably tied into many other social institutions, such as religious and economic systems. In addition, the values that pervade the social institution of mental health care in differing cultural contexts require attention. For example, seeing problems as residing within individuals as illness, as opposed to being the result of a larger social problem, is congruent with the values held in individualistic cultures.

In the contemporary West, although not generally part of the mainstream institution, significant numbers of people seek treatment for what is called mental illness through forms of faith healing, such as going to charismatic churches for exorcisms of evil spirits or praying to a divinity for healing salvation. It is increasingly recommended that Western mental health professionals align with the beliefs of their clients (Richards & Bergin, 2014). This can involve performing a thorough religious assessment and engaging in supportive practices congruent with clients' worldviews, such as joining in prayer with them and their families (if that is the client's usual practice). There are many hybrid models of such healing approaches in which various faith traditions are integrated into the delivery of mental health practices. Such models represent reconciliation of differences and realization of ways to implement inclusive, rather than divisive, approaches.

Who Is the Healer?

When Friedman consulted with a Native American tribe, there was a clear bifurcation between those who embraced Christianity and those who held onto their traditional ways. Both sides distrusted each other, as the Christian contingent tried to "save" their "heathen" brethren, while the other side berated the Christians as "apples," apostates who were red on the outside but white on the inside. The Christian group wavered between accepting so-called scientific mental health approaches and advocating faith solutions such as prayer, while those holding onto their older traditions tended to reject contemporary Western perspectives for the more traditional solutions institutionalized within their culture.

When a preteen from this tribe, who had been expelled from school for violent outbursts, was referred for psychological intervention, his family decided to avail themselves of both psychological intervention and also a traditional healing ritual that involved having the boy's maternal uncle deliver a deep scratch to the boy with a sacred eagle claw. It is noteworthy that this painful ceremony had to be administered by a related adult male, but one who was not part of the immediate living arrangement, as the pain of the ritual could cause discord within the household if administered by one living in the same residence. As the tribe's consulting psychologist, Friedman was caught between two cultural understandings. The mainstream U.S. culture undoubtedly would have seen this eagle-claw intervention as child abuse, which would require reporting to local law enforcement—and likely would result in the boy being removed from his home into "protective" custody, while the family could face criminal-justice sanctions. In addition, reporting this family would not only likely hurt the boy by removing him from his caring family and hurt the family through the ensuing legal consequences, but would deservedly cause anger in the tribe. Recognizing and respecting this ritual as something that likely had long been adaptive in this cultural setting involved taking the emic perspective of the family and its culture, and not simply imposing an etic Western understanding on the ritual. Reconciling and realizing a solution to this dilemma required complex negotiations among stakeholders, such as state law enforcement and tribal elders, which were reconciled in a way that allowed the eagle-claw ceremony to proceed, after which the boy's behavior showed considerable improvement as he wore the resulting scar with pride as a badge of honor.

CASE ANALYSIS: WOMEN ENTREPRENEURSHIP AS A FORCE FOR NATION BUILDING

Women at the Forefront of Change

Mobilizing women entrepreneurs for advancing economic development in war-torn and postconflict countries has become an increasing social movement. Many Rwandan women entrepreneurs, like their African sisters and global counterparts, are at the forefront of a well-documented trend to advance gender equality and promote economic growth and nation-building. One compelling difference in the Rwandan circumstance is the ever-present shadow cast by the genocide of 1994. Although not often a topic of open discourse within Rwanda, the genocide permeates the culture, as Rwanda is a nation of survivors. The women are resourceful, persistent, and determined that this will never happen again. Rwandan women entrepreneurs who graduated from a Peace Through Business (PTB) entrepreneurship-training program see entrepreneurship as critical to nation-building, and the best way to advance the Rwandan economy through the private sector. In this sense, they see nation-building in post-genocide Rwanda as an enterprise with a bottom line focused on gender equality.

Prior to the genocide, Rwandan women's voices were barely heard, but postgenocide women represent 70% of the Rwandan population (Mirzoeff, 2005). Rwanda is committed to building a private sector for its devastated economy through entrepreneurship led by its women (Traoré, Gonzalez, Yedro, Lobet, & Bailey, 2013). The "Voices of Women

Entrepreneurs" report issued by the International Finance Corporation (2008) indicated that women's participation in the Rwandan labor force is at almost 80%, with women comprising 58% of enterprises in the informal sector (p. 10).

The Folly of a One-Size-Fits-All Training Model

However, the entrepreneurship model used was primarily Western-based, an American model focusing on skill-building, cash-flow management, marketing, and client-service tools applicable to a different economy. Recent development work conducted within Rwanda by our colleague, Nancy Coldham, has focused on listening to the voices of women enterprise leaders to create sustainable entrepreneurship models relevant to their local culture. Her development initiative began when she engaged 30 graduates of a Peace Through Business program conducted in Rwanda in 2012. She applied participatory action research, informed by feminist, post-Colonial, and empowerment theory, to work with these women entrepreneurs to customize this to the local culture.

Empowerment became a goal and a legacy of Nancy's work. Empowerment as a goal is about having control over determinants of one's quality of life, whereas empowerment as a process permits the participant control or input in determining the goals undertaken (Tengland, 2008). Prescribed development often appears to be charity, but empowered development, particularly with women entrepreneurship, became a lesson in feminist participatory action.

Nancy applied a transcultural lens to hear the voices of the Rwandan women entrepreneurs, ensuring that the training and mentoring models were culturally relevant and not "one size fits all." She focused on the issues around translating a Western-styled entrepreneurship training program for women into postgenocide Rwanda from the perspective of three main questions: How could entrepreneurship training and mentoring best be structured and delivered to meet the needs of Rwandan women entrepreneurs? What is the value or impact of women entrepreneurship training and mentoring on increasing entrepreneurial capacity in Rwanda? Last, in what ways could women entrepreneurs contribute to Rwanda's economic renewal and nation-building as a result of being well-trained? The overall goal of her work shed light on the significance of women entrepreneurship in war-torn and postconflict countries, while considering the impact of transculturally sensitive training.

Nancy Coldham recognized and respected the differences she noticed and aimed to reconcile these through providing culturally appropriate interventions. She has remained engaged with the Rwandan entrepreneurs to enhance their potential for sustainable realization by creating a Canadian-based foundation to provide an additional source of seed capital for some of the growing enterprises. She is also working with Rwandan-inspired mentoring and an e-based entrepreneurship-learning program to spread the training and knowledge to others, exemplifying transcultural competence.

9

Avoiding Cultural Traps

Culture is adaptive . . . until its context changes so that it is no longer adaptive. (Bohannan, 1995, p. viii)

Hall (1981, p. 1) in *Beyond Culture*, stated: "Despite our faith in technology and our reliance on technological solutions, there are no technical solutions to most of the problems confronting human beings . . . until mankind transcends the intellectual limitations imposed by our institutions, our philosophies, and our cultures." In addition to the prerequisites and other guidelines we have offered for professionals who wish to become transculturally competent, we also recommend they understand the necessity for being *culturally adaptive*. Professionals who claim to be culture experts can often be observed to resist adapting to cultural changes in their environments, even when the need is staring them in the face. They may be quite content to conduct "business as usual,"

http://dx.doi.org/10.1037/14596-009
Transcultural Competence: Navigating Cultural Differences in the Global Community, by J. Glover and H. L. Friedman

regardless of the context in which they are operating, repeating in cookie-cutter fashion whatever approach might have worked in the past. Professionals who display these rigid behaviors are essentially closed to the outside, and their adaptive capacity for recognizing, respecting, reconciling, and realizing solutions to cultural differences and dilemmas is minimal, if not absent completely.

Trompenaars and Hampden-Turner (2002) described the cultural values influencing this condition as *inner-directedness.* Professionals with this value orientation are often content in their conviction that they know best. Ethnocentrism frequently is associated with such inner-directedness. Ethnocentric people make judgments about others' cultural values, systems, and behaviors on the basis of their own worldviews. They believe that their ways of doing things are superior to the ways of others who are different from them. Ethnocentrism acts as a blinder to seeing the adaptive value of others' perspectives. It is a human affliction that can be found to some degree in all societies and organizations, but it has its recent legacy in the West through Colonialism in which the temporary ascendance of Western power was wrongly generalized by many as Western culture's overall superiority to all other cultures. In rapidly changing sociocultural contexts, found now in the global community, a cultural orientation based on such ethnocentric beliefs is not conducive to transcultural competence.

THE PREVALENCE OF CULTURAL TRAPS

When Is Culture the Problem?

Bohannan (1995), in *How Culture Works*, described the irony of culture. He explained that cultural orientations and standards in past times were positive adjustments to previous contextual circumstances, but these may lose their advantage when things change; indeed, with change in either the physical or the social environment, old cultural ways can work against the very people they were devised over the generations to help. Culture may then prevent being able to see the options available for adaptive responses. When culture becomes the problem, rather than the solution to problems, it is a cultural trap. Continuing to believe in the superiority of Western cultures due to their temporary ascendency to power during Colonialism is a cultural trap.

Culture becomes maladaptive when its shared knowledge, which had helped its members to adapt to a specific environment in the past, is no longer appropriate for the current environment. An organization's culture, including the beliefs, values, and behaviors of its leaders, can even become a trap that brings about the demise of the organization.

Many culture traps surround us today, but such traps have surrounded humans in every historical era. Only if individuals and organizational leaders recognize those traps, which means understanding the ways values, actions, and beliefs turn into traps, and actively seek exits or solutions or both, can communities, corporations, governments, and other organizations flourish, or even survive, in the current global era. This also applies to the professional survival of individuals. If unable to see beyond culturally limited models for adapting to change in the face of expanding choices for new cultural orientations, cultural traps can destroy organizations and individual careers.

Bohannan (1995) explained that there is one thing we can be sure of: Just as life may create hazards that lead to its extinction, culture creates hazards for the creatures that bear it. How many faulty premises do people logically build upon that then lead them to undesirable ends? Just as mortality is built into life, so absurdity leading to extinction is built into culture. Whenever people cannot think about either their natural or social world without such crippling cultural premises, they are in a cultural trap. Cultural traps occur in human organizations when parts of a cultural tradition get hold of the human mind in a way that makes it impossible for people to separate culture from the natural (physical and biological) and social dimensions of their situation.

Scientific explanation, religious faith, political correctness—in fact, any cultural virtue—may become a cultural trap. A virtue turns into a cultural trap if people slavishly follow some specific formulation of it, and if they cannot examine and question the context and results of following their virtue. As conditions change, any religious explanations or political convictions that stifle thought and preclude questioning become deadly.

When that happens, the very culture that helped its people solve their former problems can become a trap that destroys everything their predecessors worked to achieve. Any people who are not willing to reconsider old ideas as they slip into new contexts may be doomed to live in a fatal cultural dead-end.

For those people and groups caught in cultural traps, narrow perspectives cause them not to be aware of options in their environments. If the environment, including the social environment, changes in such a way that a cultural tradition is no longer an advantage in dealing with that environment, the tradition's imperatives become the iron teeth of a cultural trap that closes tight, making further adaptation impossible.

The Inca Empire

Before European contact, the Inca Empire was one of the most powerful and wealthy in the Americas. In the 14th century, the Incas controlled a territory more than 1,500 miles long in what is now Ecuador, Peru, and Chile. The Sun King was the Inca political ruler in a highly centralized and very efficient national structure. The Sun King was also a primary deity of the Inca religion. Nation-state and religion were the same to the Inca citizens.

When newly arrived Spanish conquistadors, under the leadership of Pizarro, encountered the Inca king virtually unprotected outside the Inca capital, they were able to capture not only the king but the Inca religious deity as well. The result was an almost immediate and complete surrender of the powerful and militarily effective Inca nation to a handful of Spanish. Due to the highly centralized structure of the Inca empire, there were no alternative means of organizing and managing the society once their king and deity was removed.

Prior to the arrival of the Spanish, the Inca culture had adapted well. However, when the context changed with the introduction of the Spanish and their lack of fear and respect for the Inca, that culture lost its adaptive potential. Its past success, and all that had evolved around it, became one cause of its failure to adapt to the loss of its deity and ruler. The Incas could not overcome the void in decision making and leadership created by the capture of their leader. The Incas were caught in a cultural trap that the Spanish used, perhaps unknowingly, to their advantage.

The case of the Incas illustrates the influence that an ideology can have over a group of humans. In this case, it was an entire nation that was caught in a trap that originated from restrictions inherent to their culture. Contemporary organizations whose leaders have almost "deity-like" control may have similar experiences when those leaders leave suddenly. This practice might be able to explain the high occurrences of maladaptive situations, such as governments that remain unresponsive to citizen needs, corporations that fail to see shifts in market demands, and military commanders of "superior" forces that are defeated by enemies using "nonconventional" strategies.

Questioning premises is not easy. It creates discomfort, and people are usually loath to do it, even when they know they need to. Culture is so firmly embedded in all forms of human organization, and so slow to change on its own, that it will usually blindly perpetuate the status quo. Thus, one of the key challenges for being transculturally competent is to be able to proactively shift into alignment with the new demands of constantly evolving contexts. Unfortunately for the Inca, they were caught in a cultural trap.

SEEING THE BIG PICTURE

Transculturally competent professionals are a breed apart from those typically found in government offices, corporate boardrooms, and community meetings—even those who might be well known for their cross- and multicultural skills. Transculturally competent professionals are able to deal effectively with uncertainty in their environments, brought on by the diversity of the global community, rapid-fire technological changes, and political, social, and economic volatility.

Transculturally competent professionals avoid the cultural traps of linear and single-option perspectives. They employ proactive strategies, rather than reactive ones. Alternative futures are continuously evaluated and anticipated as future possibilities. They are able to see options and find ways to reconcile and realize solutions for cultural dilemmas.

The Swiss Watchmakers

This is exactly what did not happen in the Swiss watch industry when it failed to market the quartz watch. The Swiss had all the expertise, but they were unable to use it because the forces of the present were so very damaging for the future. By the 1960s, they had completely dominated the worldwide watch industry for 100 years. They had invented the tuning fork and the quartz movement. But they gave this technology to the United States and Japan by displaying it at a trade show. They provided these ideas to other nations rather than make use of it themselves. Watchmakers from Japan and the United States quickly seized these ideas and developed them into a new concept of timekeeping.

That failure on the part of the Swiss watchmakers was a sort of testimony to the power of inertia, the power of being successful, the power of the status quo, the power of a single culture, the power of a single set of systems and procedures that make today's goods really well but hinder tomorrow's adaptiveness. The influence of their past successes blocked their ability to adapt to the future. Instead of embracing change, they embraced the intellectual imperialism of their one-best-way model for making watches.

Transculturally competent professionals realize that they must make decisions within a greater context than their own. They realize their position and place in the grand scheme of things. They are able to operate effectively in different and varied settings, always remembering who they are and understanding the consequences of their actions. They understand that their actions may have long-term consequences for themselves, their organizations, and their planet, good and bad.

Predicting Tourism Growth in Paradise

An airline executive presented an analysis of economic growth for a small Pacific Island nation to a group of financial and accounting executives at a conference. He was the marketing vice president for a regional airline that had experienced considerable growth during the past decade.

His positive outlook for future tourism growth in the nation was supported by polished graphics illustrating growth trends from recent years.

The numbers of inbound passengers had grown in a linear fashion, and his speech left no doubt in listeners' minds that the growth would continue. After all, the government of the nation had made tourism a major focus in recent years and had committed several million dollars to advertising in global markets. Visitors raved about the beauty of the beaches and the weather. The local people were increasingly being employed in resorts and other tourism-related enterprises.

He conveyed to the audience that his airline had just completed a strategic plan, within which were plans for new aircraft to be purchased and new routes established to open important international markets. When asked by a member of the audience what the future held, the presenter could say only positive things.

Five days later a political coup replaced the government. A new government was formed to satisfy the majority ethnic group's desire for greater political representation and equal economic access. The results for tourism in the small nation were drastic. Tourists, fearing violence in the aftermath of the coup, cancelled their reservations. The airline load capacity went from 90% before the coup to 20% after it. Resort occupancy was around 20%, and some resorts even closed. The bright future described by the airline executive only 5 days before the coup was no longer in sight. Most leaders in the nation were thinking in a basic survival mode.

What was the problem with the strategic plan developed by the airline prior to the coup? It assumed that the past would predict the future. The perceptual process of the airline's leadership did not let them see what was coming. The leaders ignored the social unrest that had been signaling the possibility of a coup. In fact, they had seemed oblivious to the signals they were receiving from the community, choosing to see only their linear models and projected future as reality. Had the leaders been more open to holistic sources of data, such as the rumbling dissatisfactions that led to the coup and that did not fit their precisely modeled projections, they might have been able to develop other scenarios and responses. These leaders were not open to other possibilities due to their blinders.

In using scenarios to plan a small business, to choose an education, to look for a job, to judge an investment, or even to contemplate marriage, people need to be open to change. Often, scenarios can help people make better decisions—usually difficult decisions—that they would otherwise miss or deny.

The following case illustrates how transcultural competence is necessary in development and change initiatives. The well-intended consultants, Glover along with his team, thought they had the "answer" for the Tongan economic-development problems related to squash-pumpkin production and exports, but it was their presence, not their "expert" solution, that enabled Tongan leaders to fix the problem using their traditional cultural ways.

CASE ANALYSIS: CULTURAL INCOMPETENCE IN TONGA

In 1992, the U.S. Forest Service sponsored a national-level change project in Tonga upon request by the Tongan Department of Agriculture. The goal was to improve the quality of the squash-pumpkin exports from this Pacific Island kingdom to Japan. The initial year of producing and exporting pumpkins had been an economic windfall for the nation in 1990, but success and rapid growth in the new economic activity brought unforeseen crises. In the second year of harvesting, Japanese importers threatened to stop importing pumpkins from Tonga because 35% of shipments to Japan were being rejected due to quality problems. The Japanese importers had given the Tongan government an ultimatum: Reduce the quality problems by the next harvest or lose the contract.

Tonga, a small island nation in the South Pacific, was the last kingdom in the region. Visitors to Tonga were reminded of a more romantic and traditional island life typical of the 1950s. Villages were often still actively involved in subsistence farming and fishing, and people lived as they had for centuries. Villagers' aspirations had grown as the Tongan government had made attempts to build a cash economy. Tonga, like other dependency economies, had been looking for a way to increase its self-sufficiency, and exporting squash-pumpkins to Japan seemed to be a good way to begin that process.

In their attempts to resolve the quality issue with the pumpkin exports, the leaders of the Tongan Department of Agriculture and Fisheries (TDAF) requested assistance from various international agencies, including the U.S. Forest Service. One of the leading foresters invited us to consult, along with our colleague, Papalii Dr. Failutusi Avegalio, on the cultural issues surrounding the pumpkin-quality problem.

Stakeholders

Upon arrival in Tonga, our consulting team began to meet with the stakeholders involved with the squash-pumpkin problem. The minister of the TDAF introduced us to a wide variety of stakeholders whose roles, as well as their culturally influenced orientations and expectations in the farming and production of pumpkins, were quite diverse. The TDAF minister was a long-time government employee who appeared to enjoy the status associated with his position. He focused on the relationships of the agency with higher level Tongan leaders, including the international advisors. He understood the global economy and was a player in the decision to grow and export squash pumpkins. The TDAF deputy minister was a very well-educated official who comfortably acted as a cultural broker for us with various stakeholders in Tonga. As a deputy minister, he was actively involved in the operation of the agency. He was a driving force in our invitation to come to Tonga.

The forester was a well-intended and capable official with the U.S. Forest Service who developed the grant and funding to support our efforts. He was culturally sensitive to many of the issues we faced and assisted with our workshop sessions.

Agricultural extension agents were Tongan men who had been identified as the trainers and change agents involved in the squash-pumpkin production. They were in the "middle" since they understood both the agency's and the farmers' dilemmas. Most were open to external ideas and felt the urgency of fixing the rejection-rate problem as much as any of the stakeholders.

Farmers were village leaders. They were usually of high status in the traditional village system and held values for entrepreneurial activity. Most saw the pumpkin exporting as a way to build a better life for their village and families. Some were becoming more individualistic in their economic orientation, although they still held traditional Tongan values.

Village farmworkers were a mixed group comprised of men, women, and children who did the actual work in the fields. They were in many cases related to the farmers. Their orientation was collective, and they often held traditional Tongan values.

Exporters were local expatriate businessmen who served as middle people between the Japanese buyers and the farmers. The Tongan government regulated their activity through laws and the Ministry of Agriculture and Fisheries. Most exporters operated according to their Western values.

Shipping companies were the exporters' primary contacts in the marketing and delivery processes. They were paid the same, regardless of the pumpkin rejection rate. They too were somewhat regulated by the Tongan government while operating in the port city of Nukualofa.

Japanese buyers (importers) were very concerned that they had lost face when their Japanese business partners became aware of the pumpkin-quality problem. They had delivered the ultimatum to the Tongan government to reduce the rejects or lose the contract to export pumpkins to Japan.

International aid advisors were expatriates from Germany, New Zealand, and the United States, and were already there upon Glover's arrival. Each advisor, influenced by his or her own cultural biases, had an opinion as to how the Tongans ought to resolve the pumpkin-quality problem.

Change and Cultural Dilemmas

As our work with the Tongan pumpkin problem progressed, we discovered a number of cultural dilemmas, or seemingly opposed values among stakeholders. Not only were the proposed solutions to the quality problem numerous, but the differences were based on national, professional, and role differences among the stakeholders. Riding on the wave of a current change-methodology fad in the United States, our consulting team was well armed with participative management and continuous improvement theories. When we arrived, we quickly were made aware of the fact that everyone did not share our culturally influenced design for the solution to the pumpkin problem.

For example, a German advisor had set up a quality-control system, designed to have a number of quality inspectors at the docks where the pumpkins were delivered prior to being shipped to Japan. His perceptions of the problem and its solution were based on a linear and sequential analysis. If the problem were to be solved, the Tongans would need inspectors at the end of the Tongan production, harvesting, and delivery process to catch the rejects before they were loaded on the ships for export to Japan. As a stakeholder in the change initiative, he was convinced that his way was the correct solution to the problem.

There were other stakeholders, each with their own culturally influenced ideas about what needed to be done. An advisor from New Zealand suggested that contract farmers be brought in from the Philippines. An advisor from England suggested that the village collective social structure needed changing, and suggested identifying and training entrepreneurs, and paying them as individuals to eliminate the village hierarchy.

As change agents, Glover and his team recommended a solution to improve the processes involved in pumpkin production and exporting, from the initial planting to the eventual receipt on the dock in Japan. In other words, they believed that Tonga faced a process problem consisting of numerous small problems that could be improved, in contrast to the German advisor, who adamantly believed the best solution was to focus on controlling rejects at the end of the process. Within this process analysis, conducted through focus groups, structured interviews, and observations, Glover discovered over 50 miniprocesses that were contributing to the rejection rate.

Quality Training for Farmers

During the first year of pumpkin planting, agricultural extension agents from the TDAF had conducted numerous training programs for farmers. Well aware of the critical importance of exporting pumpkins to the nation's economic-development efforts, they had worked long and hard to assure that all of the farmers had the best knowledge of techniques for planting, harvesting, and growing pumpkins. Upon further discussions with the farmers, we discovered that they themselves did little work in the fields. The farmers were actually Tongan entrepreneurs who spent most of their time in the port, dealing with exporters, shipping schedules, and government officials. The farmers were also village leaders, with considerable ascriptive status in their local village. They used their children, wives, and lower status men from the village to do all of the actual farming. Further, Glover discovered that the farmers had not communicated the information and techniques learned in the agricultural extension training to the people who actually did the farming.

Glover asked several farmers why they attended the training if they did not do the actual work. Their responses indicated that they attended the training because it was a high-status event, appropriate for village leaders such as themselves. Glover also learned that their ascriptive status in the village often prevented them from spending time in the fields with women and children. They did not transfer their new information to those doing the actual work because it was considered low status to do so.

Pumpkin-Production Methods

Farmworkers' methods used for planting, harvesting, and packing the pumpkins were inconsistent and problematic. For example, instead of using a machete to cut the pumpkin from the stem during harvesting, they would often break off the stem by hand. This caused damage to the part of the pumpkin where the stem was attached.

Also, farmworkers would pick the pumpkins when they knew that other villages were also harvesting, without regard for when their pumpkins had been planted. Many of the pumpkins were picked before they were ready for harvest and would arrive in Japan either too small or overripe due to the collective practices of the villagers.

Quota-Based Payment Expectations

Discussions with the farmers, buyers, and shippers revealed another important process that contributed to the rejection rates. The farmers had been given the expectation that they would be paid for their harvest on the basis of the number of pumpkins delivered to the docks. The shippers were not clear on what the farmers should expect. However, Japanese buyers and Tongan government officials had agreed that the Japanese would buy only pumpkins that arrived in Japan and met rigid quality specifications for ripeness, size, and other quality considerations. This fact had not been communicated to those stakeholders below that level. Related to this quality-versus-quantity dilemma was the fact that farmers encouraged their workers to pack as many pumpkins in a shipping crate as possible. Further, farmworkers were encouraged to place the rotten pumpkins in the middle of the crate. This process, of course, resulted in the entire crate of pumpkins being contaminated by the rotten ones by the time it reached Japan.

Storage on the Docks in Tonga

Pumpkins often arrived at the dock, only to be left in the hot tropical sun for several days due to exporters' requirement that all farmers deliver their pumpkins on the same day. Since only one of the ships could be loaded in the harbor at a time, many crates stayed out in the sun until the ship moved from being anchored offshore to the dock.

Efforts Begin

After the discovery of these and other process problems based on stakeholders' unclarified assumptions, Glover and his team began a series of workshops with approximately 40 farmers, extension agents, exporters, and expatriate advisors. The first day was difficult. Tongan administrators and the forester introduced us to the group. As we explained our observations and discussed the basics of our analysis, there was almost no response from the group. Accustomed to interactive-workshop participants from the United States, we did not feel that the first morning session had gone well. However, during the morning coffee break, we could hear the participants outside, speaking in Tongan, and apparently very much involved in some sort of assessment of our earlier analysis and discussion. Then, one of the leaders of the group came back into the building. He smiled and explained that the group had discussed our presentation, and that they were interested and wanted to hear more.

By the third day, the group had become polarized in its support of either the German advisor's quality-control solution for the end product or Glover's process-improvement perspective. Both solutions for change were based on respective professional cultural orientations and predispositions for how to handle the pumpkin problem. Glover's progress on the first morning was being overshadowed by the looming debate that was festering under the surface between the sequential and linear solution of adding control inspectors at the end of production and the synchronic solution involving developing quality teams and building improvement into the miniprocesses identified throughout production.

On the morning of the fourth day, Glover noticed an air of excitement in the room as he and his team arrived. The forester told us that the prime minister of Tonga was coming to meet us for lunch. During the morning, it seemed that the group was no longer distracted by the opposing designs, and we pushed even harder for "participation" by all stakeholders in a continuous-improvement process. When the prime minister arrived, he listened carefully and then asked what the actual problems were. We explained that the training had been misdirected to the farmers instead of to those who did the actual work in the fields, that confusion existed about how farmers were to be paid for their crops, that many of the pumpkins were being picked prematurely to meet the quotas set by the exporters, and so forth. The prime minister left, and we went on with our sessions, feeling that he supported our participative approach to change. We proceeded, in typical Western consultant fashion, to "impose" our team approach to solving problems on the stakeholders.

Several months later, the minister for TDAF visited Hawaii. Glover met him for lunch, eager to know how his change approach was working. The minister proudly told him that in the recent harvest the squash-pumpkin rejection rate on the docks in Japan had been reduced from 35% to 5%! Further, he explained that when Glover left Tonga, he and the Prime Minister had met with the king and reviewed the findings regarding the faulty processes and how they were contributing to the problem. Glover also learned that the king immediately created laws to correct each of the faulty processes. The laws were implemented swiftly and effectively. The Tongan people lived in a monarchy in which autocratic decision-making was how things got done. The solutions endorsed by the king were culturally appropriate for that sociocultural context. The participative solutions Glover and his team offered were not culturally appropriate for Tongans, who solved the problem their way.

Case Discussion

The Tongan government leaders had translated most of what had been discussed with the prime minister into law without any participation in the decision-making processes by farmers, agricultural extension agents, or exporters, all of whom were told in an autocratic manner what to do. The result was dramatic. The ascriptive power of the Tongan king was obeyed by stakeholders without question. The pumpkin rejection rate had been reduced from 35% to 5% in the next harvest.

Neither Glover's solution to the problem nor the German advisor's had been effective. The ascriptive leadership of the Tongan kingdom "fixed" the pumpkin problem, and the Tongan people supported this change as the appropriate way to fix the problem. Although Glover had identified certain aspects of the problem with a process analysis, the collective-oriented Tongans, for the most part, wanted nothing to do with this version of teamwork. It was far too participatory for them. Instead, they waited politely until Glover and his team had left and then implemented change in their culturally appropriate manner.

In hindsight, we believe Glover and his consulting team should take little credit for fixing the pumpkin problem in Tonga. While he debated with the German advisor about the best way to resolve the rejection-rate problem, the Tongan hierarchy simply used their insights and put them into law, while the farmers and other stakeholders quickly adopted the prescribed solution.

Potential for Transcultural Competence

We believe that the Tongan leaders were very adaptive in their approach to change. They carefully reviewed the outsiders' different analyses and solutions, then found a way to make things happen in their culturally appropriate way. Glover's analysis of the miniprocesses, the rejection figures compiled by the German advisor, and the different designs for fixing the problem were integrated into a new way of doing things that suited the Tongans' traditional way of instituting change.

There are lessons for change leaders everywhere in the Tongan example. First of all, change always involves stakeholders with culturally prescribed ideas for what needs to be done. Second, those cultural prescriptions will most likely include opposing values of stakeholders. And finally, in every human context, there are culturally appropriate rules for how to create change, regardless of the content or goals of the change initiative.

10

Catch the Pigeon but Look out for the Wave

In this concluding chapter, we present some exemplars of transcultural competence. We have previously discussed two transculturally competent professionals, namely, Loy Weston, who built KFC Japan by reconciling two very different corporate cultures, and Yasuki Muira, former president of JAL Development in North America. And, of course, we have based much of this book on the work of Fons Trompenaars, who is an extraordinary exemplar of transcultural competence.

Although many of our professional experiences were in the Pacific Islands, they are similar to the experiences of professionals around the world. Having also worked in the Caribbean and Latin American, the United States, Europe, Asia, and Africa, we have observed the need for transculturally competent professionals everywhere. The setting does not have to be exotic and remote. Some of our best cases of cultural dilemmas come from the boardrooms of U.S. corporations. Our experiences in

http://dx.doi.org/10.1037/14596-010
Transcultural Competence: Navigating Cultural Differences in the Global Community, by J. Glover and H. L. Friedman

both domestic and international settings, including universities, militaries, governments, education systems, and health care and human services organizations, all show the need for transcultural competence.

Our work in the Pacific Islands provided us the opportunity to work with Tusi Avegalio, who provided leadership with the Tongan squash-pumpkin problem. Most of us who know and respect him simply call him "Tusi." He has reconciled his early socialization within a traditional Samoan village with his Western academic achievements, including a doctorate from the United States, and he is a model for how to operate effectively in diverse settings, ranging from corporate boardrooms to traditional village ceremonies. Tusi is the executive director of the Pacific Business Center and works to help Pacific Islanders reconcile traditional economic systems with the global marketplace. Wherever he goes, he exudes the type of charm and self-effacing humor that enables him to find adaptive ways to function, regardless of the specific context. Whether this might be due to learned skills from his multicultural background or from other factors leading to his personal charisma, his high level of transcultural competence is notable. Our attempts to rationally define what may go into such skills may provide a guide, but how any individual embodies these in a contextual way that goes beyond individual traits to becoming able to forge an adaptive fit within any cultural context is another matter. We have been fortunate to work with Tusi and many other transculturally competent colleagues in numerous corporate, government, community, and national change and development initiatives in which cultural differences were always present and the transcultural competence of our professional team was needed for success.

We would be remiss if we did not also mention our colleague Tomasi Vuelivoloni. "Tom" is a leader who built a very successful financial services company in the Pacific. When he retired as CEO from that company, he became the minister for business development in Fiji and a member of the prime minister's cabinet. Tom, along with Tusi and other leaders, including us, developed the Change Leadership Forum in Fiji, a highly successful organization whose mission is to develop leaders and organizations. Tom was transculturally competent, as he understood global business and was able to adapt to a variety of sociocultural contexts. He could be comfortable in a boardroom in Paris, yet also comfortable in his village of Raki Raki, where you might find him drinking kava and leading a discussion with the village elders on a mat under a group of palm trees.

Nancy Coldham is one more example of a transculturally competent professional. Nancy is an entrepreneur who has proven that she can adapt in a variety of cultural contexts. Her master's degree in international and intercultural communication received the Canadian Governor General's Gold Medal Award 2013 for academic excellence, and required fulfillment of an international residency requirement in which she worked with an NGO in India focused on developing women entrepreneurs. This educational requirement is something we mentioned as sorely needed in more programs training professionals to be transculturally competent. Nancy's social and charitable pursuits continue to focus on the advancement of women in business and in politics, both in Afghanistan and Rwanda, as well as in her home country of Canada. Her work in developing culturally appropriate training programs for women entrepreneurs in Rwanda demonstrated her transcultural competence and adaptive leadership.

WHAT HAVE WE LEARNED FROM OUR EXPERIENCES?

As consulting professionals, we have served prime ministers, traditional chiefs, CEOs of international companies, NGOs, villagers, and many other stakeholders. We have also worked in regions around the world in more countries than we care to count and within a variety of organizational settings, such as insurance companies, mental health facilities, schools, hospitals, oil suppliers, hotels, airlines, governments, tribes, and banks. All of our clients and partners have been seeking to create successful change in order to lead their people through the often turbulent cultural environment of recent times. The constant in our work with this diverse group of clients was, indeed, their diversity. Every project in which we were involved included a variety of stakeholders with different cultural values, and the expected cultural dilemmas accompanying such diversity. Based on those experiences, we make the following recommendations for achieving transcultural competence, which we believe can benefit any professional, anywhere in the global community.

Creating "New Boxes"

"Catch the pigeon but look out for the wave" is a traditional Samoan saying that has relevance for transcultural competence. Catching a pigeon might be a metaphor for developing new technology, building a new tourist development, or implementing a new government policy on fuel-use tax. In fact, the "pigeon" could be any goal that leaders might seek to achieve.

The "wave" might be the unforeseen consequences of a professional's decision making. The wave could represent the impact of a resort on local villagers who had been subsistence farmers. Or the wave could represent the layoff caused by new technology implemented in the workplace. The wave could be dissatisfied customers who object to the new cost-cutting telephone-answering system that does not seem to permit access to a real human voice.

If there is one catalyst for transcultural competence in individuals and their organizations, it is decision making. Adaptive and sustainable success rests with the quality and cultural appropriateness of the decisions that are made by leaders in government, community, and corporate organizations in the face of challenging dilemmas with no right or wrong answers, but that vary in their adaptive outcomes.

Contemporary leaders must be able to scan their horizons and think beyond the obvious, beyond what is known about their world. This vision must be used to create sustainable solutions that go beyond the immediate needs of a company, community, or nation. Humans have always had the need for leaders who were successful at adapting their institutions and behaviors to the world around them, whether those leaders were a group of prehistoric tribal elders deciding to move the tribe to an environment where food was more abundant or a military leader introducing a new form of warfare to gain advantage over opponents. In a more contemporary context, the transculturally competent professional might be the CEO of a computer software company initiating change by introducing a new technology into culturally diverse global markets. Or an international aid worker finding ways to bridge the cultural difference between Western-trained medical professions and local villagers. Or a corporate human resources executive from the United States who wants to implement a pay-for-performance program throughout an international company located in countries with many different motivational values. Cases such as these will most likely require reconciling and realizing cultural dilemmas to create new boxes, new ways of dealing with the dilemma that were not in the available solutions for the dilemmas prior to reconciliation. After all, reconciled solutions are required because, in the old box, the cultural designs for dealing with the problem were not obvious to the various stakeholders involved.

Know Your Cultural and Professional Baggage

Perhaps the most important thing we have learned is that professional consultants and other leaders need to adapt to the social and cultural context of wherever they might be working. The global community has many opportunities for consultants and leaders who are able to check their professional baggage, and avoid stereotyped cultural prescriptions, when they arrive. Abstract consulting models, even when bolstered by so-called scientific data and their related values, may appear to work smoothly in classroom discussions and among communications at conferences with professional peers, especially when in familiar surroundings. However, the ability to reconcile diverse stakeholders' models is needed for realizing sustainable results in the complex world of real cultural differences. Being wary of hidden biases and cultural traps is essential to being transculturally competent. Assuming that there is but one best way does not work in the Caribbean, or Africa, Asia, the Pacific, or South America. In fact, it rarely works in any area of the world.

Include the Past on the Way to the Future

It is important to understand that all people, whether traditional Pacific Islanders or participants in the New York Stock Exchange, have been adapting to change since there first were people. For example, Pacific Islanders have successfully navigated vast oceans and found cultural means to develop prosperous and sustainable societies. Unfortunately, outsiders, particularly consultants, international-aid providers, and investors in the region, often placed little value on the Pacific Islanders' cultural traditions. In our development and change initiatives in the Pacific Islands, we found that the past offered a way to successfully change, as frequently the best way to the future is through the past. Instead of devaluing the history and traditions of the Pacific Islanders, we used them as a foundation for change and development initiatives. Likewise, entering a board of directors meeting in London should be treated with the same need for understanding sociocultural context. Valuing the local culture is important wherever one might work around the world.

Reconcile Competing Models

Unfortunately, we observed many well-intended professionals who were not able to find ways to design initiatives to reconcile competing models for how the world should be. The result is often competing stakeholders and conflict between advocates of those models.

Cultural models for sustaining traditional communities and corporations are often based on relationships. Status in the traditional organization is based on position in the social system. Westerners, in particular, those who have come to the areas such as the Pacific Islands to create development and change initiatives, often bring their own models, which are often little more than cultural baggage. This baggage can compound the negative consequences of competing development and change models by not respecting traditional village and other cultures. In our work in the Pacific, we were fortunate that Tusi, with whom we frequently collaborated, has ascribed status in many of the region's traditional cultures, as well as the transcultural competence to successfully navigate implementing development and change projects.

Square Ships Don't Sail Very Well

Organizational cultures can become like square ships, unable to effectively plow through the water, as leaders are incapable of recognizing that it is the cultural design of the organization itself that prevents it from being productive and fulfilling the visions and missions of its leaders.

In our work, we often found clients who did not recognize that the issues and problems that we were asked to "fix" originated in their own organizational culture and solutions hidden by their own cultural blinders. Instead, these clients frequently found reasons to "blame" local employees and their culture. For example, workplaces in government and businesses in the Pacific Islands had often become dysfunctional combinations of Western models and traditional practices. A common dynamic is the one previously discussed of expatriate bosses promoting the young worker to supervise others in the workplace, including their elders from local villages where they hold traditional status and authority over the young workers. Imagine the life in the village of a young supervisor who has disciplined his village elders or even a chief in the workplace. Expatriate bosses may not understand why young workers frequently do not want to be promoted, and stereotype this as a lack of initiative, ignoring these basic cultural dynamics.

Transcultural Competence Involves More Than Completing a Checklist

The prerequisites for cultural understanding and application, Trompenaars's 4 Rs, and the four-step dilemma-reconciliation process together provide a valuable set of tools for professionals striving toward transcultural competence. As we learned in Tonga, change was implemented in a culturally congruent way, and our approach to facilitate this had little to do with how that change actually occurred. This demonstrates that transcultural competence involves a continuous process of adapting, and not something one can ever claim to have achieved in any final sense. However, making use of the tools we have provided may go a long way toward helping those embarking on the journey of becoming more transculturally competent.

References

Adair, J., Deuschle, K., & Barnett, C. (1988). *The people's health: Anthropology and medicine in a Navajo community.* Albuquerque: University of New Mexico Press. (Original work published 1970)

Adler, N. (1991). *International dimensions of organizational behavior* (2nd ed.). Boston, MA: PWS-Kent.

Adler, N. J., & Gundersen, A. (2008). *International dimensions of organizational behavior* (5th ed.). Mason, OH: Thomson.

American Psychological Association (2007). Guidelines for education and training at the doctoral and postdoctoral levels in consulting psychology/organizational consulting psychology. *American Psychologist*, *62*, 980–992. doi:10.1037/0003-066X.62.9.980

Barth, F. (1967). On the study of social change. *American Anthropologist*, *69*, 661–669. doi:10.1525/aa.1967.69.6.02a00020

Becher, T., & Trowler, P. (2001). *Academic tribes and territories: Intellectual enquiry and the cultures of discipline.* Philadelphia, PA: Open University.

Bernard, H. R. (2011). *Research methods in anthropology: Qualitative and quantitative approaches* (5th ed.). Lanham, MD: Altamira.

Bohannan, P. (1995). *How culture works.* New York, NY: The Free Press.

Braxton, J. M. (1995). Disciplines with an affinity for the improvement of undergraduate education. In N. Hativa & M. Marincovich (Eds.), *Disciplinary differences in teaching and learning: Implications for practice* (pp. 59–64). San Francisco, CA: Jossey-Bass. doi:10.1002/tl.37219956409

Brotherton, P. (2011, August 19). *Fons Trompenaars.* Retrieved from http://www.astd.org/Publications/Magazines/TD/TD-Archive/2011/08/Fons-Trompenaars

Collins, J., & Porras, J. (1994). *Built to last.* New York, NY: Harper Collins.

Copeland, L., & Griggs, L. (1985). *Going international: How to make friends and deal effectively in the global marketplace.* New York, NY: Random House.

Fitzgerald, F. S. (1945). *The crack up.* New York, NY: New Directions. (Original work published 1936)

Foster, L. (2009). *A brief history of Mexico.* New York, NY: Checkmark.

Friedman, H. (2009). Xenophilia as a cultural trap: Bridging the gap between transpersonal psychology and religious/spiritual traditions. *International Journal of Transpersonal Studies, 28*, 107–111.

Friedman, H., Glover, G., & Avegalio, F. (2002). The burdens of other people's models: A cultural perspective on the current Fiji crisis. *Harvard Asia Pacific Review, 6*, 86–90.

Friedman, H., Glover, G., Sims, E., Culhane, E., Guest, M., & Van Driel, M. (2013). Cross-cultural competence: Performance-based assessment and training. *Organization Development Journal, 31*(2), 18–30.

Glover, G., Friedman, H., & Jones, G. (2002). Adaptive leadership: When change is not enough—Part One. *Organization Development Journal, 20*, 15–31.

Hall, E. T. (1981). *Beyond culture.* New York, NY: Anchor. (Original work published 1976)

Hampden-Turner, C., & Trompenaars, F. (1993). *The seven cultures of capitalism: Value systems for creating wealth in the United States, Japan, Germany, France, Britain, Sweden, and the Netherlands.* New York, NY: Doubleday Business.

Henrich, J., Heine, S. J., & Norenzayan, A. (2010). The weirdest people in the world? *Behavioral and Brain Sciences, 33*, 61–83. doi:10.1017/S0140525X0999152X

Hesketh, T., & Zhu, W. X. (1997). Traditional Chinese Medicine: One country, two systems. *British Medical Journal, 315*, 115–117. doi:10.1136/bmj.315.7100.115

Hofstede, G. (2005). *Culture's consequences. Comparing values, behaviors, institutions, and organizations across nations.* Thousand Oaks, CA: Sage.

International Finance Corporation. (2008). *Voices of women entrepreneurs in Rwanda.* Washington, DC: World Bank.

Jones, B. B., & Brazzel, M. (2014). *The NTL handbook of organization development and change: Principles, practices, and perspectives.* Oxford, England: Wiley-Blackwell. doi:10.1002/9781118836170

Kuhn, T. (1962). *The structure of scientific revolutions.* Chicago, IL: University of Chicago Press.

Laurent, A. (1983). The cultural diversity of Western conceptions of management. *International Studies of Management & Organization, 13*(1/2), 75–96.

Lewin, K. (1947). Frontiers in group dynamics. In D. Cartwright (Ed.), *Field theory in social science: Selected theoretical papers by Kurt Lewin* (pp. 188–237). New York, NY: Harper & Row.

Lopez, P. D., & Ensari, N. E. (2013). Fostering multicultural and internationally competent individuals and teams. In R. L. Lowman (Ed.). *Internationalizing multiculturalism: Expanding professional competencies in a globalized world* (pp. 173–198). Washington, DC: American Psychological Association.

Lowman, R. L. (Ed.) (2002). *The California School of Organizational Studies handbook of organizational consulting psychology: A comprehensive guide to theory, skills, and techniques.* San Francisco, CA: Jossey-Bass.

Lowman, R. L. (Ed.) (2013). *Internationalizing multiculturalism: Expanding professional competencies in a globalized world.* Washington, DC: American Psychological Association.

Machinga, M., & Friedman, H. (2013). Developing transpersonal resiliency: An approach to healing and reconciliation in Zimbabwe. *International Journal of Transpersonal Studies*, *32*(2), 53–62.

Marshak, R. J. (1993). Lewin meets Confucius: A re-view of the OD model of change. *The Journal of Applied Behavioral Science*, *29*, 393–415. doi:10.1177/0021886393294002

Marx, K. (1992). *Capital: Vol. 1. A critique of political economy* (B. Fowkes, Trans.). London, England: Penguin. (Original work published 1867)

Matsumoto, D., & Van de Vijver, F. J. R. (Eds.). (2011). *Cross-cultural research methods in psychology.* New York, NY: Cambridge University Press.

Miner, H. (1956). Body ritual among the Nacirema. *American Anthropologist*, *58*, 503–507. doi:10.1525/aa.1956.58.3.02a00080

Mirzoeff, N. (2005). Rwanda and representation after genocide. *African Arts*, *38*(3), 36–96. doi:10.1162/afar.2005.38.3.36

Morrison, T., & Conoway, W. (2006). *Kiss, bow, or shake hands: The bestselling guide to doing business in more than 60 countries* (2nd ed.). Avon, MA: Adams Media.

Mukherjee, P. K. (2001). Evaluation of Indian traditional medicine. *Drug Information Journal*, *35*(2), 623–632.

Murdock, G. (1967). *Ethnographic atlas.* Pittsburgh, PA: University of Pittsburgh Press.

Polanyi, K. (1944). *The great transformation.* Boston, MA: Beacon.

Richards, P. S., & Bergin, A. E. (2014). *Handbook of psychotherapy and religious diversity* (2nd ed.). Washington, DC: American Psychological Association. doi:10.1037/14371-000

Rogers, E. M. (1983). *Diffusion of innovations.* New York, NY: Free Press. (Original work published 1962)

Sackmann, S. A. (1991). Uncovering culture in organizations. *The Journal of Applied Behavioral Science*, *27*, 295–317. doi:10.1177/0021886391273005

Sam, D. L., & Moreira, V. (2002). The mutual embeddedness of culture and mental illness. In W. J. Lonner, D. L. Dinnel, S. A. Hayes, & D. N. Sattler (Eds.), *Online readings in psychology and culture* (n.d.). Bellingham: Western Washington University Center for Cross-Cultural Research. Retrieved from http://www.wwu.edu/culture/Sam_Moreira.htm

Schein, E. H. (1992). *Organizational culture and leadership: A dynamic view.* San Francisco, CA: Jossey-Bass.

Smith, A. (1904/1776). *The wealth of nations.* London, England: Strahan. Retrieved from http://www.econlib.org/library/Smith/smWN.html

Snow, C. P. (2012). *The two cultures.* Cambridge, England: Cambridge University Press. (Original work published 1959) doi:10.1017/CBO9781139196949

Squires, G. (2005). Art, science and the professions. *Studies in Higher Education, 30*, 127–136. doi:10.1080/03075070500043077

Steward, J. H. (1972). *Theory of culture change: The methodology of multilinear evolution.* Urbana: University of Illinois Press.

Tengland, P. A. (2008). Empowerment: A conceptual discussion. *Health Care Analysis, 16*, 77–96. doi:10.1007/s10728-007-0067-3

Thurow, L. C. (1992). Who owns the twenty-first century? *Sloan Management Review.* Retrieved from http://sloanreview.mit.edu/article/who-owns-the-twentyfirst-century/

Traoré, M., Gonzalez, A., Yedro, C., Lobet, J., & Bailey, J. (2013). Rwanda: Fostering prosperity by promoting entrepreneurship. *Doing Business, 2013*, 37–41.

Triandis, H. C. (1994). *Culture and social behavior.* New York, NY: McGraw-Hill.

Trompenaars, F., & Hampden-Turner, C. (2002). *Riding the waves of culture: Understanding cultural diversity in business.* New York, NY: McGraw-Hill.

Trompenaars, F., & Woolliams, P. (2004). *Business across cultures.* Chichester, England: Wiley.

Trompenaars, F., & Woolliams, P. (2006). Cross-cultural competence: Assessment and diagnosis. *Adaptive Options, Spring*, 5–9.

Trompenaars, F. (2012). Foreword. In K. Berardo & D. Deardorff (Eds.), *Building cultural competence: Innovative activities and models* (pp. ix–xii). Sterling, VA: Stylus.

Weber, M. (1930/1905). *The Protestant ethic and the spirit of capitalism* (T. Parsons & A. Giddens, Trans.). London, England: Unwin Hyman. Retrieved from http://www.marxists.org/reference/archive/weber/protestant-ethic/

Index

About the Authors

Jerry Glover, PhD, is a cultural anthropologist who has worked in consulting, research, and education projects around the globe. He is currently an associate of Trompenaars Hampden-Turner, consulting on client projects in transcultural competence and eLearning development. Dr. Glover is a board member of the International Society for Change and Development and a peer review editor for the *Organizational Development Journal.* He has been a faculty member of the graduate program in organizational change at Hawaii Pacific University for 27 years. He earned his doctoral degree in cultural anthropology from the University of Florida in 1981. Dr. Glover's professional career includes working as a consultant on 150 change and development initiatives, including corporations, governments, and professional applications such as education, health care, military, tourism, and economic development. He has developed initiatives for transcultural competence education and training in locations such as Fiji, New Zealand, Hawaii, the Bahamas, Europe, and North America. He has conducted extensive research on organizational culture, culture change, and cultural dilemmas in sociocultural encounters. Dr. Glover has numerous publications in the fields of change, leadership, and culture.

Harris L. Friedman, PhD, consults domestically and internationally with organizations and has built a number of mental health and health care companies. He also has worked as a clinical psychologist in diverse settings.

He received his doctorate in clinical psychology from Georgia State University, and is certified in both organizational and business consulting psychology, as well as in clinical psychology, from the American Board of Professional Psychology. Dr. Friedman retired as an emeritus professor of psychology at Saybrook University and research professor of psychology at University of Florida, but he continues to research and write extensively on a wide variety of topics in psychology and related fields. His writing includes numerous articles on organizational culture, cultural dilemmas, and adaptive leadership. He is a Fellow of the American Psychological Association, senior editor of the *International Journal of Transpersonal Studies*, and associate editor of *The Humanistic Psychologist*. His most recent coedited books are *The Praeger Handbook of Social Justice and Psychology, Volumes 1–3* (2014) and *The Wiley-Blackwell Handbook of Transpersonal Psychology* (2013).

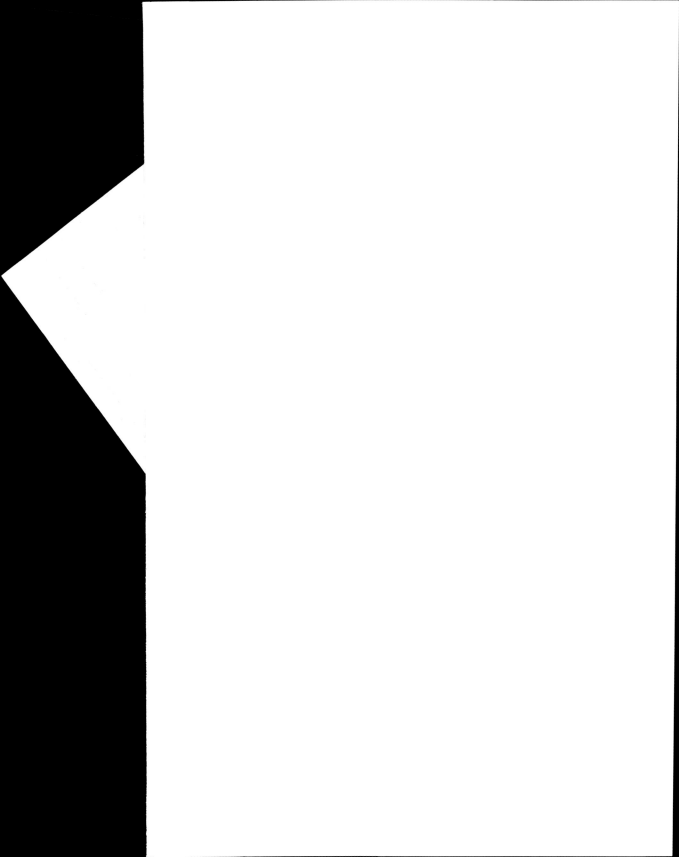

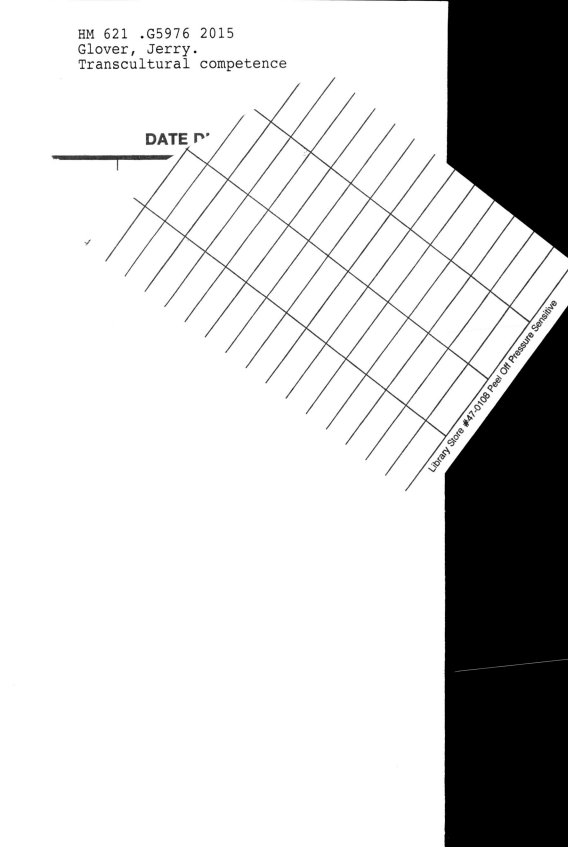